SOCIAL - TO SAVE

A Book of Suggestions
For The
Social Commitees Of Christian Endeavor
Societies And For The Home Circle

By Amos R. Wells

MANAGING EDITOR OF THE GOLDEN
RULE, AND AUTHOR OF "SOCIAL
EVENINGS," "THE JUNIOR MANUAL,"
"WAYS OS WORKING SERIES,"
"FOREMAN JENNIE," ETC.

First Fruits Press
Wilmore, Kentucky
c2015

Social--to save: a book of suggestions for the Social Committees of Christian Endeavor Societies and for the Home Circle, by Amos R. Wells.

First Fruits Press, ©2015
Previously published: Boston, Chicago: United Society of Christian Endeavor ©1895.

ISBN: 9781621714057 (print), 9781621714064 (digital)

Digital version at http://place.asburyseminary.edu/christianendeavorbooks/31/

First Fruits Press is a digital imprint of the Asbury Theological Seminary, B.L. Fisher Library. Asbury Theological Seminary is the legal owner of the material previously published by the Pentecostal Publishing Co. and reserves the right to release new editions of this material as well as new material produced by Asbury Theological Seminary. Its publications are available for noncommercial and educational uses, such as research, teaching and private study. First Fruits Press has licensed the digital version of this work under the Creative Commons Attribution Noncommercial 3.0 United States License. To view a copy of this license, visit http://creativecommons.org/licenses/by-nc/3.0/us/.

For all other uses, contact:

First Fruits Press
B.L. Fisher Library
Asbury Theological Seminary
204 N. Lexington Ave.
Wilmore, KY 40390
http://place.asburyseminary.edu/firstfruits

Wells, Amos R. (Amos Russel), 1862-1933.
   Social--to save : a book of suggestions for the Social Committees of Christian Endeavor Societies and for the Home Circle / by Amos R. Wells.
   159 pages; 21 cm.
   Wilmore, Ky.: First Fruits Press, ©2015.
   Reprint. Previously published: Boston: United Society of Christian Endeavor ©1895.
   ISBN: 9781621714057 (pbk.)
1. Amusements. I. Title.
GV1471 .W465 2015

Cover design by Jonathan Ramsay

asburyseminary.edu
800.2ASBURY
204 North Lexington Avenue
Wilmore, Kentucky 40390

First Fruits Press
The Academic Open Press of Asbury Theological Seminary
204 N. Lexington Ave., Wilmore, KY 40390
859-858-2236
first.fruits@asburyseminary.edu
asbury.to/firstfruits

SOCIAL—TO SAVE

A Book of Suggestions

FOR THE

SOCIAL COMMITTEES OF CHRISTIAN ENDEAVOR SOCIETIES AND FOR THE HOME CIRCLE

BY

AMOS R. WELLS

MANAGING EDITOR OF THE GOLDEN RULE, AND AUTHOR OF
"SOCIAL EVENINGS," "THE JUNIOR MANUAL,"
"WAYS OF WORKING SERIES,"
"FOREMAN JENNIE,"
ETC.

BOSTON AND CHICAGO
UNITED SOCIETY OF CHRISTIAN ENDEAVOR

COPYRIGHT, 1895,

BY THE

UNITED SOCIETY OF CHRISTIAN ENDEAVOR.

SOCIAL — TO SAVE.

A COMPANY of men and women were shipwrecked on an island. Death stared them in the face, — death from the hungry waves that lashed the shore, death from the hunger that lashed their fainting bodies. Wild beasts were prowling through the gloomy woods behind them, and a cold night was settling down. What did they do? The captain urged them to get together, build a fire, organize two bands, one to hunt for food while the other made a stockade for safety, and then, around the fire, safe in the stockade, the entire company would eat and drink and praise God together.

But they did none of these things. Said one, "I am too busy; don't you see I have set my stakes for a house?" Said another, "I am too bashful to go into company." Said a third, "The ship's crew are dreadfully coarse men, and really the party would better be more select." Said a fourth, "I am too tired; it will do me more good to sleep." "But it is for life," urged the captain; "for life and safety." Nevertheless, he urged in vain.

A True Picture.

You know that no such scene as this was ever on earth? Would you were right! For indeed I have only pictured to you in a figure precisely what is happening every month in thousands of our Christian churches. Shipwrecked companies are we, cast up on these strange shores of time out of the vast ocean of eternity, with death and that ocean impatiently awaiting us, and hunger at our hearts, and the night coming down, and the beasts in the woods. And our Captain urges us, for life, for safety, to live for one another; to gather around the same camp fire; to give the reassuring pressure of the hand and clasp of arm about the neck; to drive away by love the wild beast of loneliness, and by friendly merriment the ghost of gloom. "Be social— to save," cries our Captain. But we have no time. And we are too bashful. And we abhor disagreeable people. And we want our own set. And it does not come easy. And we are too tired with our day's work. And there will be enough without us.

O, Endeavorers, when I think of that wide, mysterious sea upon which I must soon embark alone, alone — till "I shall meet my Pilot face to face," I do not want to set sail from a lonely hut while my brothers are wandering in the forest, I do not want to put forth from a silent shore into the silent sea. I want the banks to be thronged with people clasping hands, and I want a great, glad shout to speed me onward: "Good bye, brother! Only a day or two, and we shall all be with you again!"

"Social" Defined.

What is it to be social? It is to appreciate the meaning of life. It is to realize that we are set here in this world, not for houses, lands, gold, silks, praise, authority, fame, but for character. It is to put first the kingdom of God, and his righteousness.

Gold separates men. They sneak off, each to his own gulch, jealous lest some one else should preempt a valuable claim before he does. Ambition separates men. My brother and I cannot both hold the office at the same time, and therefore — well, "Heaven helps him that helps himself." (Some think that is in the Bible!) Spite of trusts and combines, of clubs and cliques, the god of this world is a god of division, of isolation, and it is only as men get into their souls the love of God and the thought of his eternity and theirs, that permanently and truly they draw nigh to one another.

How to be Winsome.

I want to emphasize this truth, because failure to understand it is at the bottom of all our social failures, in the Christian Endeavor society and everywhere else. Do you want to be social? Do you desire the charm of winsomeness, that will draw men and women to you, as bees to the sweetest of flowers, as eyes to the loveliest sunrise? The secret of it does not lie in small talk, or jokes, or animal spirits. You do not need beauty, or wit, or learning. A dancing master cannot give it to you, nor a professor of etiquette. The secret of loveliness is the love of Christ. The secret of winsomeness is the desire to win souls for the Master. You cannot be social until you are social — to save.

Do not mistake sparkle for sociability. The iceberg sparkles. Do not mistake movement and animation for sociability. The ice cold waves that fret the coast of Labrador are full of most impetuous life, but they encrust everything with icicles. You may make a great stir about socials in your Christian Endeavor society, but unless the warm heart of Christ is in them, your socials will be more like the water of Labrador than the water of life.

Good — Better.

Etiquette is good, but Christ is better. Unless, to win souls to Christ, you are willing to transgress the laws of etiquette, — to speak without an introduction, for instance, — you cannot be social. Good manners are good, but Christ is better. Unless, to win souls to Christ, you are willing to meet uncultured people, clownish people, disagreeable people, you cannot be social. Industry is good, and the desire to get on in the world, but Christ is better. Unless, to win souls to him, you are willing to take time from your business, and get on a little less rapidly in your studies, your bank account, your reputation-building, you cannot be social. A knowledge of one's self is good, but Christ is better. Unless, to win men to the Master, you are willing at least to try to forget self, to lose self-consciousness in service, you cannot be social.

A Recipe.

The spirit of snobbishness will kill the socials of any society. Christ would not be admitted today into certain circles of so-called Christians, if he came in the working clothes of a carpenter. Good socials must be democratic, and the washerwoman's daughter and ashman's son must be made to feel as much at home as the daughter of Senator Biggun or the son of General Moneybags. Egotism, the feeling that you are better than other people, either on account of a better filled purse, or because of a better filled head, or because of some other gift of fortune or industry, will destroy any social, — does kill every social that is dead at all. Put in place of this contemptible spirit the humble acknowledgment of sinfulness and unworthiness, and the glad perception that all for whom Christ died are brothers and sisters in him, and you will have, you cannot help having, successful socials. I do not much care what games you play or whether you play at all; what refreshments you serve, or whether you let the over-burdened stomach alone and serve none at all; sociability does not consist in forms and trappings, but in the spirit. Forget yourselves; remember Christ; seek to win friends for him : that is my recipe for a good social. *Forget yourselves; remember Christ; seek to win souls for him.*

What a farce is a Christian Endeavor society that is not social! A *society* not *social*, — what a contradiction in terms! Some are not societies at all, but *separieties*, — mere collections of self-centred ones. And this society of ours is an *Endeavor* society, — endeavoring, at any rate, to be social. Moreover, it is a *Christian* Endeavor society, — trying to be social after the pattern of Christ, after the fearless, brotherly, loving pattern of Christ. And it is a *Young People's* Christian Endeavor society, and so should be free from the class distinctions, the caste spirit, the artificial barriers, that obtain out in the world, but that have not yet parted young Christians from one another, and, please God, never shall.

Saving Souls.

How can we expect to save souls except by being social? Our lips are not eloquent to preach or plead, nor our hands skilled to push the pen along lines of power. We cannot preach Christ, but we can smile Christ. We cannot argue men into the kingdom, but we can sympathize them in, we can love them in. Are you a hermit Christian? Do you belong to a hermit Christian Endeavor society? There is a little mollusk that bores its way into limestone, makes a cell, enlarges it as itself grows, and speedily manufactures its own tomb, becoming many times too large to get through the narrow opening by which it bored its way in. Precisely this is the folly of every Christian and of every Christian Endeavor society that is not social, that does not go out into the highways and hedges, throw loving arms around the ugly, the stupid, the ragged, the wretched, and compel them to come in.

Know Thyself.

Let alone a knowledge of Christ, and of Christ's children, how can we get a knowledge of ourselves unless we are social? You think you believe in the brotherhood of man. Test yourself at the next social, and see whether you do not practically believe only in the brotherhood of the congenial. You think you trust in Christ. Test the matter at the next social, and see if you can trust him even in so slight a matter as overcoming diffidence and awkwardness. You think you are unselfish. Make trial of it at the social by forgetting whether you are having a good time in your desire to give a good time to others. Social intercourse is the touchstone that will try your gold, and without it your religion is likely to be just fool's gold, and you never know it.

The Communion of Saints.

The vast majority of Christian Endeavorers are church members, and take part in the sacred communion service. Did you ever think that this is not merely a communion with Christ, but with one another? The ancient Christians did not forget it, as they went breaking bread from house to house. Hosts of savage foes raged without. It was never known what sad gaps would be found at the next meeting,—gaps made by the cross, the lions, the sword, the fire. Do you not think they knew every strange face at those communion tables, and when a man or woman joined the church then, in the face of that terror and hatred and yawning death, don't you think he got a welcome? And don't you think the other church members recognized him on the street the next day?

I sometimes wonder that God does not send upon

his church some great calamity, to teach us what we have well nigh forgotten, the communion of saints. In our creeds we say we believe it, and then go on and let the secret societies, with their grips and passwords, excel us in the enthusiasm of brotherhood, in *esprit de corps*. Endeavorers, in your acquaintanceships and friendships is it practically immaterial to you whether a man, a woman, is a Christian or not? In your business and your politics, on the street, in the office, and in society, does your heart go out equally to Christian and non-Christian? Is there to your eyes any practical, decisive line of demarcation between Christian society and society that is not Christian? If not, then no wonder you care little for Christian Endeavor socials. How an old soldier rejoices to meet his regimental comrades! How an Odd-fellow fraternizes with another Odd-fellow! How two Icelanders, met together in New York, almost fall on each other's neck! Shall we admit any tie of nation, race, or organization to be as strong as the " tie that binds our hearts in Christian love?" And yet we find it difficult, sometimes, to hold Christian Endeavor socials!

A Stint.

What is it that is the great barrier to Christian work? We do not know one another well enough. We are afraid of one another. Smith is sure by his downcast expression that Jones is in trouble, but he does not go to his aid because he fears he will offend him. O we need, Endeavorers, we sorely need to get within helping distance of one another. Within hearing distance, within touching distance — that is easy; but many live all their lives in the same house and never get within helping distance. Now I declare that if your socials did this for you, putting you on terms of genuine, mutual helpfulness with your friends, they would be as valuable as your prayer meetings, and as acceptable to Christ. Why can they *not* do this for you?

I propose to you a stint: that at your next social you try faithfully to leap over the barriers of reserve that keep you out of some one life. Knock down the ice-wall of formality, push through the thorny hedge of disagreeableness. dash across the moat of shrinking climb up the slippery bank of awkwardness, in some way, in any way, storm the castle, penetrate its labyrinths, get within helping distance of some one soul. And if you pick out the most lonely and least attractive person in the room, and if it takes several socials to win the victory, all the sweeter will be the triumph, and the warmer the approval of our Elder Brother. Only by such personal work as this, in our socials, can we become soul-winners. Only thus can we conquer our gawkishness, our diffidence, our clumsiness. Only thus, moreover, can we gain confidence and power in our prayer meetings, because in no other way can we learn our brothers' needs, that the prayer meeting should help, and conquer our fear of our brother, so that we shall venture to help him. And thus there is no better ally of the prayer meeting than the social.

As it is in Heaven.

For another reason, too, the social and the prayer meeting should go hand in hand. "Gospel" means "good news." "Evangelism" means the same thing. Joy is at the foundation of religion. It is easy to be good when we are merry. Laughter is not only one of the best gymnastics of the body; it strengthens and invigorates character. The reason why some Christians do not grow in grace is because they don't have fun enough. More hearty joking often means more hearty praying.

Why, we are to have society in heaven, are we not? — and societies, too; Christian Endeavor societies, for all I know. And what society that will be! No wall flowers there, but everybody eagerly out in the midst of things. No waiting for introductions there, with the glorious new name on our foreheads. Everybody interested in everybody else. No one bored or stupid or shy. All faces bright and beaming. Social committees, while you are about your tasks that are often severe and perplexing, rest on the thought that it is for this society you are training the other members and yourselves. "He who loves not his brother whom he has seen, how can he love God whom he has not seen?" He who is not sociable here, how can he expect to enjoy the society of heaven?

What kind of sociability have they in heaven? The answer to that question may tell us how to carry on our socials here below.

Four Kinds of Times.

Well, for one thing, I am quite sure that they have a good time. You may know that there are four kinds of times, — a good time, a goody-goody time, a bad time, and a baddy-baddy time. A bad time — you all know what that is. A baddy-baddy time is, for instance, a social where silly, profitless games are played, like the kissing games now happily obsolete. A goody-goody time is an over-proper time, a social that is dry and unattractive, where the games have no snap to them and the amusement does not amuse. But in heaven we shall have *good* times, and so we should in our Christian Endeavor socials here on earth. A good time is attractive enough to take everybody out of himself, and cheery enough to make every one feel happy.

The Presence of Christ.

How shall we get this kind of time? Well, to add another point to the account of the socials they must be holding in heaven, Christ will be there. He should be present from beginning to end of every Christian Endeavor social. We do not pray half enough over our socials, either while we are planning them or while we are carrying them out. Unless a social is a sort of silent prayer meeting, it is certain to be a failure. And the chief thing we should pray for is that Christ should be there. Have you read Dr. Gordon's book, "When Christ Came to Church"? Read it, and it will move you profoundly, and will open your eyes, perhaps, to see our blessed Lord in the midst of his people, when they are playing as well as when they are praying.

How if the Carpenter, dropping saw and hammer from weary hands, should in visible form enter your next social? should ask, "What are you playing, my children?" should beg, "Let me join in your game"? Would you wish the game something different? Would you like to change the spirit in which the game is played? This consideration affords the only possible answer to the common question, What games are proper for Christian Endeavor socials? The answer is, Any game in which Christ would join, — the loving, the pure, the manly, the joyous Christ.

Talking or Conversing.

I am not at all sure, however, but our social committees are likely to attach too much importance to games. There is one thing I know we are to do in our socials in heaven that we do far too seldom in our socials on earth — converse. Conversation is, I am afraid, a lost art. Indeed, has it ever been, for the majority of people, a found art? We talk, — O yes, we talk; but talking is not conversing. Talk is when Mr. Smith says something about himself, and then Mr. Jones says something about himself, in reply to which Mr. Smith tells something more about himself, in return for which Mr. Jones imparts further information regarding himself. That is talk. It gets nowhere. There is nothing mutual about it, except mutual boredom. Mr. Smith does not listen to what Mr. Jones says about himself, nor Mr. Jones to what Mr. Smith says about himself.

True conversation, on the contrary, is not a firing at cross purposes. It may be personal, but it is not egotistic and gossippy. It has one goal and one direction, and not two goals in two opposite directions. If you want to converse — and every Christian should, for it is one of the very best ways of preaching Christ, being the way Christ himself most often used — if you want to converse, you must first of all find some common interest between you and your comrade. The Christian way to do this is to discover what he is interested in, and then make up your mind to be interested in it also. Every one is most likely to be interested in what he is doing, and so I advise all members of social committees, when in doubt how to keep up a conversation with a stranger, to ask all sorts of questions about his occupation. No matter what it is. If he tends horses, develop a devouring hunger for information on horses, and currycombs, and glanders, and holdbacks, and whiffletrees, and horseshoe nails. If you are sharp, before long you will discover in his talk about horses something else in which he is interested, and you can go on to talk about that.

Put Yourself in His Place.

To converse, Endeavorers, requires sympathy more than anything else, — that sympathetic imagination which puts one's self in another's place, sees life through his eyes, joins him in his interests. And that is why true conversation is so valuable spiritually. It takes us out of ourselves, immensely widens our experiences, and deepens our knowledge, and adds to our lives the lives of those we meet. We should have far more conversation in our socials than we have.

But of course I would not depreciate games. I count a good game one of earth's chief blessings, sent from heaven. I would have all social committees hunt for them as for precious stones. There are few ways in which consecrated ingenuity can be more blessedly used than in the contrivance of bright, jolly recreations. Only, don't be too ingenious. For a safeguard, and to disarm criticism, submit to your pastor all your plans for entertainment, and admit to the social no form of amusement on which he cannot pronounce his benediction at the end.

Why Socials Lose Interest.

And then — for I must stop somewhere — there is just one other point in which our socials should imitate the society of heaven: on earth, as in heaven, the central word should be Salvation. Do you want to know why some socials lose interest? The social committee does its best. Every plan that promises diversion is eagerly taken up, and carried out with wit and grace. Every novelty is tried. Money is not stinted. There is food for the mind as well as tidbits for the palate. There are pretty decorations and pretty dresses and pretty cards of invitation.

And yet the attendance is small and constantly growing smaller. Why is it?

It is because your socials lack an adequate purpose. It is because they appeal only to the senses and not to the soul, and other less pure amusements can appeal to the senses far more successfully than Christian Endeavor socials. No; if our socials are to compete with any hope of triumph against card table and theatre and ballroom and poolroom, they must present a motive to which those cannot attain, they must be all alive with the purpose to save.

Social — To Save.

Social — to save! To save from what? Well, from loneliness, for one thing. The social committee has come to the kingdom to be the everlasting foe to cliques, and sets, and selfishness. It will seek to make the unpopular popular, by changing either his character or the character of those that snub him.

Social — to save from discontent. "Down with snobbery!" cries every true social committee. Make every one contented in his lot by respecting him in it, provided he is doing his best. Permit no caste — except the cast-iron pledge!

Social — to save from uselessness. Take the awkward boobies and transform them into wide-awake gentlemen. Develop latent talents and energies. Cultivate the wall-flowers, — the social committee is a flower committee as well, — cultivate the wall-flowers, as a skilled gardener would, until they have become more hardy plants, and can stand, without a prop, in the centre of the garden. Are you waiting for men to come half way to meet you? Go more than half way to meet men; go all the way, as Christ did.

Social — to save from gloom. If the lookout committee has done its duty, you have gathered into your society the depressed young people, the discouraged, those whose tempers have become soured. Ah, who has greater need than they of our cheery brotherhood? And yet how easy it is to let them alone, and have to do only with sunnier dispositions! But we must not let the Juniors have a monopoly of the sunshine committee, and our social workers must remember that the one test of those that "scatter sunshine" is — not whether they brighten the places already bright, but whether they shed light in the dark corners.

Social — to save from sin. I am convinced that Christian young men and women do not have enough to do with the "toughs," the disreputables. How far you should invite them to your socials depends on circumstances, — depends on the stability of character of your members. That matter your pastor alone should decide. But Christians dare not forget that Christ came not to save the righteous, but sinners; and that the disciple should be as his Lord.

Social by Proxy.

The trouble with some socials is that most of the Endeavorers think they can be social by deputy. A stranger is present at the meeting. "O, Miss Saunders will greet the stranger all right." A new family moves into the neighborhood. "O, Miss Saunders will call on them all right." An awkward boy joins the society. "O, Miss Saunders will make him feel at home." Now this is unfair to Miss Saunders, and disastrous to the society, and absolutely ruinous to yourself. As well send Miss Saunders into a gymnasium for you and say, "O, Miss Saunders will develop my biceps all right," as expect Miss Saunders to do the Christian work God wants you to do. Most societies have one or two good handshakers, tacitly deputized to do the hand-shaking for the other sixty or eighty. A stranger comes in, and if the deputy handshaker is not there, not being omnipresent, the stranger skulks to a seat, and shivers.

Everybody Social.

Brethren, sisters, the work of a social committee is not done till *all* the Endeavorers are social. Brotherliness cannot be delegated. Get the Endeavorers to see what a serious and pressing matter this is. Why, suppose the astronomers, after careful calculation, should assure us that a comet was going to strike this earth next week with such force as to destroy all life upon it. Would your society appoint a committee to do all the talking on this subject? If a stranger had a newspaper in his hand, would you wait for an introduction before you asked him the latest news from the observatory? No; every tongue would be wagging eagerly, no one would dream of being bashful, wallflowers would be absolutely unknown, were a comet to strike the earth next week. What embraces of friends! What pleadings with sinners! What frankness and hot urgency of speech!

Now why can we not feel this way all the time? Compared with the vast stretch of age-long eternity whose instants are æons, our life on earth is far less than a week. Only tomorrow, as some day we shall count time, and we shall be transferred to a new existence. We do not pass this way again. Whatever encouragement we are to give the downcast must be quickly given; whatever cheer to the gloomy, faith to the doubting, friendship to the lonely. There will be glorious sociability in heaven, but those with whom God means us to be social now may not be there, or, more likely, *we* shall not be there ourselves, scornfully having thrust aside the manifest work God gives us to do on earth. Thus I would have you plead, social committees, having in mind the eternal years, until all members of your society come to understand the responsibility of contiguity, that nearness is a divine trust, that it is for high and lasting ends that God brings human lives into contact with their own. Never rest, until all the Endeavorers are social.

Social all the Time.

And not only must all the Endeavorers be social, but they must be social at all times. Do you know, the test of a social committee comes, not in the social, but the day after; nor in the Sunday evening meeting, to which you may have welcomed the stranger heartily, but on the street and in the cars Monday morning. Why is it that people look so different in church that they cannot be recognized out of church? Do the Sunday-go-to-meeting clothes do it? Or have we partitioned our church life and our secular life off into different rooms, and locked the door between? Endeavorers, the soul-saving spirit that cannot get past Sunday midnight will never get a convert. Christian Endeavor socials are merely to set the stitches, and the solid knitting together of life to life must go on after the social is all over, or else the stitches will all be dropped.

You have more friends already, you say, than you have time for; more acquaintances than you can keep up; more calls than you can return. Very likely God wants you, in that case, to neglect your pleasant, well-provided-for friends, in favor of people less agreeable but more lonely, and sadly in need of Christian comradeship. The calls that God calls you to make are more important than a whole card-case full of unanswered calls that he does not urge you to answer.

Too Much Trouble.

It will take time and trouble to follow up all these casual acquaintances made at the Christian Endeavor socials. Of course it will. If it did not, I should not urge it, for all good things are made of time and trouble.

A farmer once hired a man to work in his potato

patch. One day he sent him out there. "John, you may attend, today, to that south field of potatoes." "But I haven't time," said John; "I've got to whittle out a toy for my boy." "I hired you to tend my potato patch, and not to make toys," answered his master. "But it's too much trouble," yawned John. "Then it's going to be too much trouble for me to pay you," replied his master. "Potato bugs'll get the crop, anyhow," urged John. "And I'll get a new hired man," murmured his master.

Now you think that all very silly stuff, because you know no hired man on earth would talk that way about work his master paid him to do; but when our Master asks us to cultivate *people*, that's just the way we talk: "No time, and it's too much trouble, and it won't pay, anyhow!"

Our Father's Business.

What *do* we consider, practically consider, our business in this world? Christ said he came to do his Father's business, and so he always had time to sit down by wells and by the wayside and stand in fields and turn aside to private houses, in order to let a little more brightness and truth into some life. He did not seek out the pleasant people. It would have been delightful for him to tarry all those three years with Mary and Martha and Lazarus, or, for that matter, to ascend with Moses and Elijah from the Mount of Transfiguration. But he had his Father's business to do.

And so have we. That business is not to have a good time, though it brings a good time; it is not to study, though it makes us wise; it is not to heap up stores of goods, though it does lay up priceless treasures. That business is not to enjoy the friendship of good people, bright people, attractive people, though it blesses us with such friendship in spite of ourselves. Our business is to spread Christ's joy among men. Our business is to be social — to save.

Oh, we need to learn how to smile, — not on our lovers, our friends, the dear ones in our homes, — we know that already; but on the peevish, the cross, the sullen, the ugly. Oh, we need to learn how to talk, — not with the friendly, the well-informed, the responsive, — we know that already; but with the stupid, the rude, the uncultured and coarse. Oh, we need to learn how to shake hands, — not with soft hands, and white hands, and warm hands, and strong hands, — we know that already; but with soiled hands, and cold hands, and hard hands, and flabby hands. Christ's hands were hard, and many a time were cold. And we need to learn the etiquette of heaven, which counts a want that we can fill the highest introduction; and we need to learn the politeness of Paradise, that bows reverently before God's image in the human form, no matter how sadly sin has defaced it. And we need the ingenious boldness of Paul, that was ready to be all things to all men, if by all means he might save one man. May God grant wit to the brains of his servants, tact to their hearts, and warmth to their hands!

SOCIALS AND GAMES.

A WORD OF ACKNOWLEDGMENT.

OF course very few of the games mentioned in the following pages are original with me. I have gathered them from all sorts of sources, books and periodicals, but mainly from the kind correspondents of *The Golden Rule*, whose contributions to its "Merry Times" department have been helpful, and greatly appreciated.

In many places I have acknowledged my debt to others for plans and suggestions, but by no means in all cases, since for many I have lost the record, or the game was discovered in some paper that itself had copied it without credit. Besides, a large number of these games I have developed merely from hints here and there, a sentence or two, or simply the title of some social reported, but not described, in the Christian Endeavor columns of some religious paper. Many other games I have also greatly enlarged or decidedly changed, to adapt them more completely to the needs of young people's societies.

NOUNS AND ADJECTIVES.

GIVE to each member of the company one of the twenty-six letters of the alphabet, going around the alphabet more than once, if necessary. Let each player then write upon a piece of paper a noun and an adjective, both beginning with the letter assigned him. The slips must be thrown into a hat, and the players will draw them out, each getting a slip other than his own. Pencils and drawing paper being furnished the company, each must proceed to illustrate his noun and adjective in one drawing. If, for example, "chair, cowardly," were the combination, a picture might be drawn of a girl standing on a chair terrified at a mouse.

HANGING.

The game of "hanging," though simple in principle, is not at all easy to play, and is very fruitful of interest and instruction. If there is a large party, in order to play this game it should be broken up into groups of three or four.

One person in each group thinks of some proverb or familiar quotation. Suppose he chooses, "Make hay while the sun shines." He marks on a piece of paper, putting a little dash in the place of every letter, and vertical lines between the words. His comrades are to find out what quotation he has thought of in the following manner.

They call for the insertion of letters one a time. Naturally they call first for *e*, since *e* is the commonest letter. The paper will then look like this: —

- - - e | - - - | - - - - e | - - e | - - - | - - - - e -

Next they may call for *i, a, o.*

When the call for *o* is made, the player with the paper, since the letter *o* is not contained in the proverb, will write it across the horizontal bar of a large scaffold that he has drawn, from which is hanging a man at the end of a rope. When a second letter has similarly been called for that is not contained in the quotation, that letter is written across the rope, and when a third letter is called for, that letter is written across the man, and the players are said to be hanged, that is, defeated in the game. If the sentence is made out before this direful event, the person who thought of the proverb is himself defeated.

TROLLEY PARTIES.

THE present fashion of holding trolley parties may well be utilized by Christian Endeavor societies, and much social pleasure as well a great deal of incidental profit may be gained from these swift rides among the pleasant suburbs of a city.

A Christian Endeavor trolley party should always have a purpose in view. For example, you may take the society out to hold a meeting in some district where a Christian Endeavor meeting would be a rare privilege, in some old folks' home, for example, or schoolhouse, or orphan's asylum.

If your city is rich with historical memories, as are most of the great cities of the country, a trolley party planned along the lines of local history, and guided in each car by some one who is familiar with the ground to be covered, and can give a running lecture upon the great events that took place near the road traversed, would prove a great success.

SIGNIFICANT INITIALS.

To play this game one of the company must think of the initials of the name of some famous man, and must substitute for his name words descriptive of the man, and having the same initials. For example, he may say, "Union general," leaving the other players to guess that he intends Ulysses Grant. After this name has been guessed, the other persons, taking turns, furnish their puzzles.

AVERAGES.

To play the game of averages successfully requires some rare qualities. The members of the party must have some wit, some ingenuity, and a great deal of good nature. This last requirement will be seen to be especially necessary.

First, the company agree upon a set of ten characteristics in regard to which they will average each other up. The list may read much like this: Brightness, beauty, politeness, courage, honesty, etc.

Each of the company is then investigated in order, and his average determined. As to courage, for instance, the person under review will lay as large claims as he can hope to substantiate, and in a jesting fashion the other members of the group will either advocate his claims or strive to bring down his average by relating stories of times when he showed the white feather. The discussion merrily goes on until the entire company is ready to vote on a per cent. A majority vote decides what shall be the rating of each contestant in regard to each quality. The player who is found, on the conclusion of the arguments, to have the largest total of per cents, is considered the victor.

A VIOLET SOCIAL.

LET the social committee prepare beforehand pretty violet-tinted cards. On each are written, in gold ink, verses of Scripture. The cards are then to be cut in two diagonally, and little bits of white ribbon may be tied in one corner.

When the guests arrive, each receives one of these halves, care being taken that half of each card goes to a gentleman, and the corresponding half to a lady. The first part of the social is occupied by matching the cards.

Those that receive halves of the same card take lunch together. At this lunch, violet tissue napkins will be used, and bunches of violets will be given to all the company. The recitation of poems on the violet, such as Lowell's, would be an appropriate feature of the evening. There may be a paper on the violet, giving stories connected with it, historical or otherwise.

INVITATIONS TO POVERTY SOCIALS.

IN "Social Evenings" I have described the plan of a poverty social. Here is an invitation to such a social that is so bright it is well worth preservation. It should, of course, be printed on coarse brown paper.

Y. P. S. C. E.

Harde Times Soshul.

You air axed to a doins us folks air a goin to hav at the hum of Mr. and Mrs. J. A. Parsons,

Friday Evenin, March 30.

RULES AND REGULASHUNS.

Chapter 1. Every woman who kums must ware a kaliker dress and apern, or somethin ekaly approperate, and leve their poughdle dorg to hum.

Chapter 2. Every gent must ware thare old close and flannil shirts. No gent with a biled shirt an dude koller will be aloud to kum onless he pays a fine uv 5 cents.

A VOTE UV THANKS

Will be given to the man or woman hevin the worst-lookin rig in the rume. These rules will be inforced to the letter. A kompetent komitee will interduce strangers and look arter bashful fellers.

EXTRY GOOD KAUGHPHY AND WRINGERS

Will be et from ate to ten o'klock. Admishun to get in will be ten cts. This takes in the supper and the hull thing.

FINES FUR LADIES.

No apurn, 1 cent ; ear rings (plane), 1 cent ; ear rings (dimund), 2 cents ; wool dress (old), 2 cents ; trimed apurn, 2 cents ; gold fraim glasses, 2 cents ; finger rings (plane), 2 cents ; finger rings (dimund), 3 cents ; wool dress (new), 5 cents ; bokey (korsaige), 5 cents ; bokey (hand), $1.00.

FINES FUR MEN.

Iled hare er wacksed mustash, 1 cent; blacked butes, 1 cent; sigars in pocket, 1 cent each sigar; pipes exemt; watches (not Waterberry), 1 cent; stove-pipe hat, 1 cent; chuing gum, 1 cent; brocade ties, 1 cent; klerical ties, 1 cent; kerrying a kane, 1 cent; stand-up kollars, 2 cents; patent letter shuse, 2 cents; died mustash, 3 cents; buttenhole bokey, 5 cents. For gent or boy with curled hair, 1 cent.

FERN SOCIALS.

THESE are exceedingly pretty affairs, and are easily got up. The announcement cards may be ornamented with pressed ferns. The room should be decorated with ferns and pretty wild flowers. The table, if there is a lunch, may be made very beautiful with ferns and moss, miniature pools of water being represented by mirrors. The entertainment may consist of quiet games, with music. Have some one recite the poem, "The Pressed Fern."

COUNTING THE WORDS.

A PLEASANT occupation for a few minutes, that may be engaged in by a large company, is the following. It looks simple, but it is not so simple as it looks. Let some one read aloud half a page from a book, pronouncing the words with moderate rapidity. As he reads, let the members of the company try to count his words. The person who comes the nearest to the truth in his estimate is judged the victor. It is astonishing how widely these estimates will vary.

ANIMATED PORTRAITS

A PLEASANT game for a Christian Endeavor social is thus prepared. Over a door drape a curtain, in the centre of which is hung a frame, through which can be thrust the heads of various persons chosen from those present. These heads are to be attired in such fashion as to represent various well-known characters, such as Christopher Columbus, Queen Victoria, Captain Kidd, Lydia E. Pinkham, etc. The audience are to be informed that they are at liberty to make frank criticisms on these animated pictures, for the purpose of causing a smile. In case the audience is successful within a certain time, the person who represents the picture must pay a fine.

CORN SOCIALS.

THE room, of course, will be decorated with cornstalks and ears of corn. Visitors to the Agricultural Building of the World's Fair will know what a fine decorative effect may be produced even by the unassuming corncob. The lunch, if you have one, will consist of preparations from corn, such as blancmange, corn-starch cake, popcorn balls, and loose popcorn. At one social of the kind of which I have heard, each guest had at his plate, as a souvenir, a corn plaster tied with a pretty ribbon! The young women received small ones, and the young men large ones.

You may have a guessing contest for part of the evening, the contestants striving to guess the number of grains of popcorn in a small dish. The appropriate prize will be a wall rack made by screwing three toilet hooks in a great ear of white corn hung by a silk ribbon.

Some one might read a paper describing different kinds of corn, — their growth, their distribution, and their value. Another might tell what kinds of substances are manufactured from corn, while a third could recite Sidney Lanier's beautiful poem, "Corn."

A CHALK TALK.

Many of your societies may contain very fair artists, who with a little encouragement will be able to set before you, possibly not such an entertainment as Frank Beard would give you, and yet an amusing and profitable chalk talk.

The plans your home artist will form for himself will be better than any I could propose. Take as a suggestion, however, one chalk talk given by an amateur before his society, and well received by them. He made a series of sketches illustrating, in a punning fashion, the names of about a dozen books, such as "Looking Backward," "Ships that Pass in the Night," "Uncle Tom's Cabin," "The House of Seven Gables," and "Rose in Bloom." As he exhibited the sketches, he gave also a comic lecture introducing each of them, and knitting them together in a loosely woven story.

The listeners were furnished with slips of paper and pencils, and required to write the name of each story as it was illustrated. The best of these lists of guesses was rewarded with a little memento.

PIGEON.

The leader of the game whispers to each one of the company the name of a bird. He then says that he will give the names of two birds together, and those two birds must change places (the company having previously been seated in a circle). When, however, he calls "pigeon" among the birds, the other members must try to catch the pigeon, a prize being given to the successful one, and the pigeon receiving the prize if no one catches it.

All but six or seven of the company are named pigeon. To blind the players, the leader calls first the names of these in pairs. These change places as their names are called. Then the leader calls, "Pigeon," and all to whom he has given that name make a frantic effort to escape from some imaginary pursuer, thinking that the whole roomful is chasing them.

A game somewhat similiar to the foregoing is described in "Social Evenings" under the title, "Pansy."

TO FIT.

An excellent amusement for a Christian Endeavor social, to fill up a spare half hour, is the following. Cut a square opening in a pasteboard, which is placed prominently in the front of the room. Distribute to the members corks of different sizes. Provide with sharp knives those that are not already provided. Explain that the task before them is to cut the corks so that they will fit the square opening, without measuring the opening, judging entirely by the eye. The one whose cork fits the best should receive honorable mention.

TOASTS.

It is a pleasant habit for a society to signalize its anniversary by a little banquet. The materials may be slight and inexpensive, — sandwiches, lemonade, home-made cake, apples, grapes, and similar easily prepared and cheaply obtained viands.

One of the pleasantest features of these annual entertainments should be the toasts. Distinguish between these after-dinner speeches and the more formal reports of the business meeting. Possibly the best idea of the character such a set of speeches should take on may be gained from the following announcement of toasts on a Christian Endeavor menu card. Notice the use of quotations from Shakespeare : —

Looking C. E. from the Administration Building,
By the President.
"*When to the session of sweet, silent thought,
I summon up remembrance of things past.*"

Society Gossip,   By the Secretary.
"*I'll play the eavesdropper.*"

Rocks and Snags,   By the Treasurer.
"*There is no living with them nor without them.*"

Searchlight Corps,   Chairman of Lookout Committee.
"*Pointing you out what thing you are.*"

The Arsenal,   Chairman of Prayer-meeting Committee.
"*And Satan trembles when he sees
The weakest saint upon his knees.*"

Your Money or Your Life,
Chairman of Missionary Committee.
"*And they all, with one consent, began to make excuse.*"
Chords and Discords, Chairman of Music Committee.
"*The man that hath no music in himself,
Nor is not moved with concord of sweet sounds,
Is fit for treasons, stratagems, and spoils.*"
Buds, Chairman of Junior Committee.
"*Rosebuds set with little wilful thorns.*"
Flowers, Chairman of Flower Committee.
"*Stars that in earth's firmament do shine.*"
The Plaisance, Chairman of Social Committee.
"*Pleasures, or wrong or rightly understood,
Our greatest evil, or our greatest good.*"
The Fish Commission,
Chairman of Society Enlargement Committee.
"*There are as good fish in the sea as ever were caught.*"
The Court of Honor, An Honorary Member.
"*Let none presume
To wear an undeserved dignity.*"

PATIENCE.

THIS game may be played by any number, provided the social committee are willing to prepare the materials. Each player must be provided with four sets of cardboard disks one inch square, each set consisting of thirteen disks, bearing in their centre the figures from 1 to 13 made very distinctly.

At the outset of the game the players must arrange their disks in thirteen piles, on tables, or on large books held in their laps. Each pile contains four figures, all alike.

One player, who is the leader, does not arrange his

disks, but throws them into a receptacle from which they can be drawn haphazard. As the leader draws his disk, he calls out its number. Each player must then take a disk of corresponding number from his piles, and move it to one of four new piles that he starts elsewhere upon the table. The disks in these four piles must not be placed one upon the other, but overlapping, so that all figures composing the pile can be seen at a glance. As each 1 is drawn, that disk is placed in still another pile, and made the basis of a final pile of thirteen ascending in regular order. Those that complete, or come nearest to completing, in this way, four piles of thirteen each, are the victors in the game.

The lowest disks in each of the four miscellaneous piles may be transferred to the four final piles as opportunity occurs. For example, if the four miscellaneous piles should end in 2, 3, 4, and 5, and a 1 should be drawn, it would be possible to form a final pile as far as five. If the removal of any disk discloses a figure next higher than can be fitted to any of the final piles, this transfer may be made, any number of disks being transferred in one play.

This sounds complicated, but it is perfectly simple when you play it. Of course the skill comes in the arrangement of the four heterogeneous piles. So far as possible, the higher numbers that will be needed at the end must be placed at the top of the rows, and care must be taken not to cut off a disk of lower denomination by one of higher rank that cannot be withdrawn.

When you have played this game a short time, you will see that a comparatively slight element of chance enters into it, and a great deal of forethought and skilful playing. Besides, it is a game that will amuse equally all persons in a large company.

A HALLOWEEN SOCIAL PROGRAMME.

IN "Social Evenings," I have described the method of carrying on a Halloween social. Here is part of a programme for such a social, that you may like to use.

HALLOWEEN SOCIAL.

C.......................... Church.

F............... Evening.

*"Come spend wi' us a happy nicht,
And crack a joke thegither."*

At the C.......................Church, ... evening. Remember it is "Witches' Night," and dinna be fley'd gin ye should see weird figures about the ingle, an' see strange faces lookin' at ye from a nook in the wa'.

PROGRAMME.

1. Music — Vocal Duet.
2. Origin of Halloween.
3. Reading — "Witches' Night."
4. Recitation.
5. A Poem in Prose.
6. Apple Gathering.
7. Refreshments, Collection, Social, etc.

EVERYBODY COME.

THE HIDDEN PAPER.

TAKE a square of white paper measuring two inches each way, and let some one go into a room apart, and place it in clear view. Then call in the company, and bid them find it. It is astonishing how long this will often take. I have known a party of twenty, each possessed of ordinarily bright eyes, to look for three-quarters of an hour before they discovered the elusive bit of paper, twisted in the rattan of a chair! As each gets sight of the paper, he must quietly seat himself.

FORTUNE-TELLING.

WHETHER fortune-telling produces amusement or not depends entirely upon the wit of the fortune-teller. If he is not ready with his tongue, it is best to have the fortunes written out beforehand. A very successful half-hour's entertainment in this line may be prepared by writing upon slips of paper quotations from the poets, describing different fates or characters.

Dress the fortune-teller in any fantastic garb you have at hand. Let him step forth from a mysterious recess hidden by a curtain, and make an introductory speech in any jargon he can muster, introducing, if he will, the names of some of the persons present, with a word or two of English conveying a sly hit.

With a profound bow he retires behind the curtain, and one after another is led forward and thrusts a trembling hand through an aperture. The wizard, with many grunts and splutterings of his fantastic dialect, pretends to read the lines of the hand, and at fast breaks out in some appropriate rhyme, which he has in the mean time been selecting. It should be stated that the person who leads up the victims announces in a whisper to the wizard each time he withdraws the name of the person who is next to be produced, so that he has an opportunity to select an appropriate fortune.

CITY CHAINS.

PLACE the players in two groups facing each other. Each group must choose a leader, with whom the members of his side communicate in whispers. In the centre is an umpire, who, with his watch, gives each side a quarter of a minute, or less, for their response.

The leader of one side begins by naming a city, such as New York. Within the prescribed time, the leader of the opposite side must name a city beginning with the last letter of New York, as Kalamazoo; and so it proceeds, each leader using the wits of all in his group to assist his own.

When a leader fails to respond in time, the opposite leader chooses one player from his opponent's side, and in his turn starts a new chain. The game can be played also with the names of famous persons, but this is harder.

THE RUNAWAY FEATHER.

PLACE the chairs in a circle, and give the players a large sheet which they will stretch tightly in their hands, holding it on a level with their mouths. A small feather, colored red or some other distinct hue, is placed in the middle. One player stands outside the ring, and as those that hold the sheet blow the feather from one to another, this outside player tries to catch it. The person nearest whom he catches it must take his place outside the circle, and attempt in his turn to seize the elusive bit of down.

What with puffing and with laughing, this sport soon exhausts the breath of the company. If the number at your social is large enough, two or more sheets should be put in requisition at the same time.

EASILY PREPARED REFRESHMENTS.

A SOCIAL committee of which I have heard, not wishing to take the usual trouble in preparing refreshments for their social, made small tissue-paper boats, tied them neatly with paper ribbons, and served a boatful of confectionery to all who were present.

A MEMORY GAME.

IN order to play this game successfully, it is necessary that the list of words and sentences given below be in the memory of one of the players, who acts as leader. This leader, turning to his next neighbor, remarks, "One old owl." He turns to *his* neighbor, and gives the same formula. So it passes around the circle till it comes to the leader again, who repeats it, and adds the formula, "Two tantalizing tame toads."

So again it goes around, and again, and each time the leader adds a new formula, until the whole is repeated, up to ten. It is safe to say, however, that no society will ever get that far. All who forget part of the formula are dropped from the circle. Here is the whole : —

One old owl.
Two tantalizing tame toads.
Three tremulous, tremendous, terrible tadpoles.
Four fat, fussy, frivolous, fantastic fellows.
Five flaming, flapping, flamingoes fishing for frogs.
Six silver-tongued, saturnine senators standing, stentoriously shouting, "So-so."
Seven serene seraphs, soaring swiftly sunward, singing, "Say, sisters."
Eight elderly, energetic, effusive, erudite, enterprising editors eagerly eating elderberries.
Nine nice, neat, notable, neighborly nautical, nodding nabobs nearing northern Normandy.
Ten tall, torn, tattered, tearful, turbulent tramps, talking tumultuously through tin trumpets.

AN EGG SOCIAL.

This social, to be successful, should have for its main feature an egg supper. The menu cards should be shaped like an egg, and the eggs themselves may be served boiled, fried, potted, scrambled, pickled, devilled, as an omelet, etc. Let the waiters wear egg-shaped aprons, the smaller end turned up. These aprons may be decorated with embroidered eggs or chickens.

The salt cellars may be made of halves of egg shells, glued to two wishbones. Egg shells may be transformed into pepper boxes, the end of each shell being sealed up by a bit of pasteboard previously perforated.

Such a social as this should be held at Easter time, when Easter eggs and Easter souvenirs, cards, etc., may be for sale.

To close the evening, carry out an egg programme that may be printed on the other side of the menu cards. This will consist of short, chatty papers on Easter eggs and other Easter symbols, such as the lily and rabbit, the Easter Monday celebrations like the egg-rolling at our national capital, and the recitations of poems on eggs.

A NEW MEMBERS' SOCIAL.

IF your society has recently had any special accession of new members, why not hold a social for their benefit? Call it a "new members' social," and urge the old members to make it their especial task on that evening to become acquainted with the new members and make them feel at home in the society.

POST.

THIS game may be played in a large hall, or out of doors on the lawn. It is especially adapted to the Juniors, and may be so played as to teach them a great deal of missionary geography. The leader either marks with chalk, or indicates with his fingers, the outlines of some mission country. Let it be India, for example. A rough triangle is fixed, and the places of the prominent mission stations are indicated by marks, sticks, stones, bushes, or trees, and at each of these places one of the players is stationed. One player might stand at Calcutta, one at Bombay, one at Madras, one at Madura, one at Delhi, etc.

The leader then takes upon himself the name of some prominent missionary of India,— say Bishop Thoburn; then, declaring that Bishop Thoburn wants to go from Calcutta to Madras, he attempts to reach one of those stations while the two occupants thereof are rapidly changing places. If he succeed in doing this, the player left out has to take his place as Bishop Thoburn, and in this way the game proceeds.

A BLIND MENU.

IF you have refreshments at your next social, try a "blind menu" for the purpose of provoking mirth. A caricature of a man's head may be placed on top of the menu, labelled underneath, "General Bill O'Fare." Below, place numbers from one to twelve. Each person present is permitted to check off, as his order, any six of these numbers he chooses, giving the card to the waiter, who will return with a tray bearing his selection. The complete bill of fare is: 1. Coffee. 2. Sugar. 3. Dried Beef. 4. Sweet crackers. 5. Soda wafers. 6. Apricots. 7. Prunes. 8. Dried apples. 9. Gingersnaps. 10. Raisins. 11. Doughnuts. 12. Toothpicks.

CHRISTIAN ENDEAVOR PICNICS.

DURING the summer, Christian Endeavor unions will miss a good opportunity for binding the societies together if they do not conduct a Christian Endeavor picnic. The social features of such an occasion may be exceedingly useful. Let every one wear his badge, stating not merely his church, but the committee on which he works. A short programme might be arranged, followed by a basket dinner. The spiritual advantages of such a meeting, if it is properly planned, may be made as manifest as the social advantages.

A BURLESQUE BANQUET.

THE point of this banquet is to serve all the viands in exceedingly small quantities. The sandwiches, for example, will be about an inch square; the pickles will be cut in very small pieces; the cheese in half-inch cubes. Bits of cake may be cut into pieces an inch square. For fruit, inch sections of bananas; for nuts, one filbert, shelled, to each person, or one peanut. The candy might be one red-pepper drop to a person. Sherbert and lemonade could be served in teacups holding about two tea-spoonfuls. Each guest could be given a little tin plate and a paper napkin.

If an elaborate menu card is printed, from which the banquet is to be ordered, the burlesque will be all the more striking. Humorous speeches should close the feast.

A ST. PATRICK'S DAY SOCIAL.

THIS must be held, of course, on St. Patrick's Day, March 17. Every one is to wear green, dressing in that color as completely as possible. Let the clover leaf have an important part in the decorations. Papers about St. Patrick and Ireland, Irish songs, and recitation of Irish poems, will furnish part of the entertainment of the evening. A great deal of sport may be gained from a competition in the telling of Irish jokes, judges being set to decide who tells the best joke in the best way. The first item in the list of refreshments of the evening may be roasted Irish potatoes, eaten with spoons from the skin.

A WAR AND PEACE SOCIAL.

DRAPE the room with the national flag, and with red, white and blue streamers. Muskets, knapsacks, cannon balls, and possibly a cannon, if you are fortunate enough to have access to one, will add to the military effect of the decorations. For the refreshments you may have soldier's hardtack, softened with lemonade.

For souvenirs you may have small flags in which may be rolled slips of paper containing conundrums. These will be given to the young men, while corresponding flags containing the answers will be given to the young 'women, and part of the amusement of the evening will consist in matching the two.

A bugler will call the meeting together by sounding the assembly. War songs may then be sung, and there may be declamations, essays, and talks, concerning war. Be sure to include in these a talk on the evils of war, and on what Christianity is doing to usher in the reign of universal peace. Give this topic to your strongest speaker, and make it the climax of the evening. Pictures may be shown, and possibly a magic lantern exhibition may be got up. The entertainment may close with taps, when the lights may be turned down for an instant. Old soldiers will help you by giving you "camp fire talks."

A HUSKING-BEE.

SOCIETIES will get much amusement out of an old-fashioned husking-bee. The older members of the church should also be asked to join. Hold a contest as to who can shell the most corn in a given time, the evidence of skill being the possession of the corn-cobs. After the frolic about the corn, the members may adjourn to the house, where appropriate refreshments will be pumpkin pies, apples, lemonade, and the like.

"D. B. F."

A LITTLE amusement for the opening of a social may be obtained in the following way. As the company enter the room, give each a card bearing certain mysterious initials. Every one is furnished with a pencil, and must endeavor to get as many as possible to sign his card, each one that signs writing a guess at the meaning of the mystic letters. It should be told the company at the outset that the letters have a direct bearing on the purpose of the social. These letters should be such as the following: T. T. E. O., "Talk to each other," D. B. F., "Don't be formal," B. A., "Become acquainted," and so on. After the company have all arrived, the chairman of the social committee will call for the various guesses as to the meaning of these letters, and much fun will be the result.

SOCIALS AND GAMES.

AN OLD-TIME SOCIAL.

REQUIRE every member to appear in old-fashioned costume. Failures may be punished with a fine of ten cents, and some, of course, will prefer to pay this fine. Instruct the members to ransack their garrets and dusty trunks for garments. For entertainment you may have talks on the costumes of fifty and a hundred years ago. Some of these talks may be given by the old people of the church. For refreshments you may have old-fashioned fare. A table of curios from Revolutionary days may be got together. Old-fashioned pictures may adorn the wall, and an old people's choir may be induced to sing some of the songs of long ago.

A QUARTETTE SOCIAL.

GIVE out cards each bearing a line of music. The cards will have been made in sets of fours, the four cards of each set containing the same line. The cards must be numbered, and the four who hold cards similarly numbered must go together to practice their line of music. At a given signal these quartettes will step in turn before the company to sing. A set of judges previously appointed will award some suitable recognition to the best quartette, probably requiring them to sing an encore! In addition to this a good programme of music may be prepared.

CLOTHES-PINS.

PLACE members of the party in two long rows facing each other. At the head of each row on a chair is a pile of clothes-pins, the two piles containing the same number. As the word is given, the head of each line picks up a clothes-pin and passes it to his neighbor, who passes it to his, and so on, no person being skipped. As they reach the end of the line, the clothes-pins are laid upon chairs placed there, and so it continues until all the clothes-pins have thus been transferred. Instantly the movement begins in the other direction, and the clothes-pins are returned to the first chairs. The side that first completes the transfer is counted victorious.

A more amusing form of this game is to require the entire pile of clothes-pins to be grasped at once, passed down the line, and then returned. If any one drops a clothes-pin he must wait to pick it up before he can hand the bundle to his neighbor. Bean bags may be substituted for the clothes-pins, or corn-cobs, wooden blocks, croquet balls, or anything else hard to handle and hold.

WHERE WERE YOU BORN?

REQUIRE the members to attend the social bearing about their clothing some plain indication of the State in which each was born. The majority of societies will contain representatives from a large number of States, so shifting is our population, and so common is travel. One born in Connecticut, for example, might wear a wooden nutmeg somewhere about her dress. A gold crown on the head might signify a native of the Empire State. A native of the Buckeye State might carry a branch from the buckeye tree, or from the horse-chestnut tree, whose leaves are almost identical.

Give to each of the company a blank piece of cardboard and a pencil, and let all make a list, as complete as possible, of the members present, writing after each name his guess as to the State where the member was born. After half an hour has been given to this, let the members one by one rise as their names are called, and tell what State they were born in, and how they indicated the State by what they carried. The members will then count up and see who has the largest list of correct guesses.

A pleasant feature of the evening will be to ask each member to be prepared to give some recitation connected with his State, or tell some pleasant story or some interesting fact regarding it.

A WOODEN SOCIAL.

THIS social is appropriately held on the fifth anniversary of the formation of the society. Questions and answers about plants and trees are to be written on chips of wood. Each Endeavorer receives a question as he enters the room, while to the strangers present, as far as the strangers will go around, the answers are given. The first part of the evening is spent in a hunt for the purpose of matching question and answer.

Then may come a programme of pleasant essays and talks on the different remarkable woods of the world. Specimens of these woods may be shown, and pictures of the trees may be exhibited. The room may be decorated with blossoms and branches of different kinds of trees. There may also be an exhibition of the products of various trees. Have songs like, " Woodman, spare that tree !"

Of course some one will present a sketch of the first five years of your society, if this social celebrates its fifth anniversary.

A POLYGLOT SOCIAL.

Decorate the room with the colors and flags of the various countries. Find out how large a stock of languages can be represented from among the members of your society and their friends, and get some kind of exercise, either song, reading, or recitation, in each language or dialect. Obtain as many natives of the countries represented as possible. If you are near or in a large city, there will be no difficulty here. Have performances on the characteristic musical instruments of the different countries. A medley of national airs may be played or sung. Urge the members that speak foreign languages to practice conversation in these tongues !

SOMETHING FROM ALL.

A pleasant game suitable for a large party and therefore helpful in Christian Endeavor socials is this : Let each member of the company write upon a slip of paper something that he desires some one else to do to amuse the company, such as, sing a song, tell a story, repeat a poem, tell a joke, and the like. These slips of paper are then collected, placed in a hat, shaken up, and each one of the players draws his fate. The leader calls upon the others to perform in turn. Of course it will be permissible for the members to exchange duties.

THE AUTHORS' EXCHANGE.

THE social committee should select as many authors' names as there will be participants in the game. If eighty contestants are expected, choose eighty authors' names, and give to each contestant eighty slips of paper, each slip having upon it the name of one author. Be sure that no player has two slips bearing the same name.

At the opening of the contest state plainly how long it is to continue, say for half an hour, and then proceed to explain the rules of the game, which are as follows: —

1. The winner of the contest will be the person who, at the end of the stated time, holds the most slips bearing the name of any one author.

2. No one is to receive the gift of a slip, but any one may exchange one or more slips with any one else present.

3. As many slips must always be given as are received, on the principle that a fair exchange is no robbery.

4. It is permissible to take more than one name to start with, though in the end only one can be counted.

This game, for which I am indebted to Mr. William W. Hunter, of Boston, is a very social one, as it requires every player to speak to every other

A MOVE.

WHERE a social consists of a musical or literary entertainment and the members are all seated, it is an admirable plan at a certain point in the proceedings to stop and require the members to move, taking up their positions for the remainder of the programme at least twenty feet from where they were first sitting, thus breaking up cliques, and putting every one present in new surroundings.

A FLORAL LOVE TALE.

DISTRIBUTE among the members of the society slips of paper containing the following puzzle. Each of the twenty questions must be answered by the name of a flower, and the social committee will give due honor to the member whose list is most complete and accurate.

A Floral Love Tale.

1. The maiden's name and color of her hair.
2. An adjective that suited her, and her brother's name.
3. His favorite sport in winter.
4. His favorite musical instrument.
5. The hour he awakened his father playing upon it.
6. What his father gave him in punishment for it.
7. What this made the boy do.
8. The name of his sister's young man and what he wrote it with.
9. What he, being single, often lost.
10. What candies did he bring to Mary?

11. What did he do when he popped the question one fall day?
12. What ghastly trophy did he offer her?
13. What did she say to him as he knelt before her?
14. What flowers did she give him?
15. To whom did she refer him?
16. What minister married them?
17. What did John say when leaving her one day?
18. What was she during his absence?
19. What fragrant letter did he send her?
20. What shall we wish for them in conclusion?

The solution of the enigmas is the following: —

1. Marigold.
2. Sweet William.
3. Snowball.
4. Trumpet.
5. Four o'clock.
6. Goldenrod.
7. Hops.
8. Jonquil (John-quill).
9. Bachelor's button.
10. Buttercups.
11. Aster.
12. Bleeding-heart.
13. Johnny-jump-up.
14. Tulips (two lips).
15. Poppy, or old man.
16. Jack in the pulpit.
17. Forget-me-not.
18. Mourning bride.
19. Sweet P.
20. Live-for-ever.

A HOLMES SOCIAL.

A HOLMES social may be carried on very easily, bearing in mind not only the genial Autocrat of the breakfast table, but also, by a pun on his name, representing different kinds of homes by means of tableaux. There will be readings from Dr. Holmes's works, and possibly a brief paper on his life; but interspersed among these will be tableaux, showing the home of the young married couple, the home of the drunkard, the Christian home, the miser's home, and the like. Possibly quotations from Dr. Holmes's writings may be found, to fit each kind of home depicted.

A STAMP SOCIAL.

ADMISSION to this social consists of twenty-five cancelled stamps. If any one desires, however, he may, in lieu of the stamps, pay an equal number of pennies. These stamps are to be used for missionary purposes, being sold to stamp-dealers. The value of the collection will be greatly enhanced if members are asked to look up their old letters at home, and the letters of their fathers and mothers, and make the collection as large and valuable as possible. The entertainment of the evening may very pleasantly be connected with stamps, especially if there are any in the society who are familiar with the many interesting facts connected with these fascinating bits of paper. By all means have an exhibition of all the stamp albums in the community.

SOCIALS AND GAMES.

A TRIP ON THE NO-NAME LINE.

HAVE platform scales in the room, and require every Endeavo er to be weighed, and to pay, as his admission to the supper, one cent for every twenty pounds of his weight. In addition, there is to be given him a ticket for an excursion on the "No-Name Line." This line has eleven stations (and others may be added), all of which must be passed before the refreshment table can be reached. The following are the stations: —

1. The City of Brotherly Love.
2. The city built on seven hills.
3. The Monumental City.
4. The Flour City.
5. The home of Mrs. O'Leary's cow.
6. The most densely populated city in the world.
7. The Crescent City.
8. The Queen of the Lakes.
9. The Modern Athens.
10. The City of Magnificent Distances.
11. The City of Churches.

Before a traveller is permitted to pass through one station to the next, the name of the station must be registered on his ticket, and the ticket must be submitted to some member of the social committee for verification. This member will write his name on the space following the name of the station on the ticket. In case the member is unable to discover the name of the station he pays a fine of one-half cent, the total fines recorded on his card being paid at the last station.

A DRAWING CONTEST.

A DRAWING contest will make an agreeable feature of any Christian Endeavor social. As the members enter, furnish each with three sheets of drawing-paper and a pencil. Set them in groups about small tables. Announce that the amateur artists will be permitted to choose their own subjects, and that each drawing must be finished within ten minutes, at the close of which the drawings will be collected and a new set entered upon.

Each drawing must be signed with the name of the artist, and the name of the person or thing he intended to depict. Judges will be appointed who will decide for each set which is the best and which is the worst drawing.

While the others are at work, these judges will hang the drawings about the room, and on the conclusion of the third set there will be a general examination of them, the members voting which drawing, in their opinion, is worthy of the highest honor, and which is the poorest. It will be interesting to see whether the common judgment agrees with the opinion of the judges. This contest may or may not be enlivened by prizes.

A SOCIAL TO SERVE.

WE have had socials of all possible descriptions: "pink socials," "peanut socials," "Scotch socials," and socials with no name at all. One thing, it may be fairly said, has been true of all that we have held. They have been for ourselves, or for other young people of the same standing in society as ourselves. Why not try a social that will mean, first of all, pleasure for those who know little of pleasure, and an abundance of hard, but delightful, work for us? In other words, have a social for the boys and girls of what men are pleased to call the lower class of society.

If your society is located in a city, it will be an especially easy matter to gather in a score, or a half-hundred, of boys and girls who do not attend religious services, and who have few chances for genuine pleasure. Let each member of the society promise to devote himself exclusively to the interest of your humble guests. Serve refreshments, play games, and in all things let the utmost informality prevail. A stirring gospel song and a prayer would fittingly close the evening's exercises. Try this, and you will surely vote it one of the most successful socials that you have ever held.

ENDEAVOR ORATORY.

A PLEASANT evening may be spent by any Endeavor society in an oratorical contest. This should be announced beforehand, and those who compete may make as elaborate preparations as they desire. It will be more amusing, however, if no previous announcement is made, but all are required to contest with impromptu speeches upon themes furnished them as they stand before the society. These themes may be placed in sealed envelopes from which the candidate will select one at random.

A POST-OFFICE SOCIAL.

A POST-OFFICE social will prove interesting. Its chief feature is the distribution of the mail, with all sorts of attendant features that may be devised by an ingenious committee. A certain number of the letters are to contain orders for various packages, which will be distributed at the Christian Endeavor express office. Both letters and packages are to be more comical than serious, though the scheme affords a fine opportunity for giving useful hints regarding societ·· methods. Nothing of a personal nature should, of course, be permitted. It will assist the fun if the members be requested to read their letters aloud in turn.

A PIE SOCIAL.

THE main feature of this social may be a large pan of bran, covered over with paper so arranged as to look like pie crust. A slice may be cut out, and so a place made where hands can be slipped in, the members withdrawing from the pie, as it is passed, pieces of paper. Upon these papers are written bright gems of thought and clever jokes. As many of these jokes as possible should be on pies. The reading of these papers is called for by number, and a few pieces of music are interspersed. Here are sample witticisms : —

" Why are we here? To cultivate ' pie-ty.' "

" What is the only kind of pie we have not on the bill of fare? Ask —— " (name of a member who is a practical printer).

SOCIALS AND GAMES. 57

A boy suggests the following menu for a dinner in courses: —

First Course.
Custard-pie with tarts.

Second Course.
Huckleberry-pie, mince-pie,
Lemon-pie, chicken-pie.

Third Course.
Cream-pie, apple-pie with cheese.

Dessert.
Pie.

An appropriate conclusion to the entertainment will be pieces of pie, passed around for the practical testing of their contents. For further ideas see " Pie Social " in " Social Evenings."

A POLITICAL SOCIAL.

FIRST the delegates are to be registered by a comical judge, who asks funny questions about the name, age, color, etc. The answers are recorded in a book by clerks. When all have registered, announce the names of political parties, Free Silver, Free Wool, Free Lunch. The Endeavorers divide themselves into these parties, each of which adjourns to a separate room.

Here, going through with the regular forms, each party nominates its candidates for such offices as dog-catcher, city hash inspector, pound-master, janitor of court-house, etc. Party platforms are adopted, and then the separate divisions adjourn to meet in one large mass-meeting.

Here, representatives of each party present before the society their candidates and platform. At the close the delegates vote in voting-booths, a complete list of the candidates being posted in each booth. Stump speeches, of course, can be made *ad libitum* in the course of the evening, and campaign processions will form part of the fun.

This social is suggested by Mrs. J. Carrie Clark.

NUMBER GROUPS.

GIVE each person present a number, printed in large type on a card which is pinned conspicuously on the breast. The numbers range from 10 to 24, and so of course there will be many duplicates. There is a leader, who begins the game by calling in a loud voice some number, such as 180. Immediately the players as rapidly as possible arrange themselves is groups, seeking to form a group the sum of whose numbers will equal 180. As soon as a group has been thus formed it presents itself to the leader, and to each member of this successful group is given a slip of paper.

As soon as one group has thus formed 180 and been rewarded, the half-formed groups are dissolved, since they do not count anything, and the leader calls out a new number. After this has been tried a certain number of times, the person that has received the largest number of slips is adjudged the winner. If you want to make this game very difficult, use higher numbers, and attach them to the backs, instead of the fronts, of the members.

THE COMMITTEES TAKE TURNS.

IF in your society the social committee gets tired, try the plan of holding committee socials; socials, that is, superintended by the different committees in turn. The slight emulation that will be provoked will result in the best socials your society has ever held.

A VEGETABLE SOCIAL.

HAVING previously announced what will be expected of the members, let the social committee set at the door of the room capacious baskets for the reception of gifts of vegetables which the members will bring for the use of the poor of the town.

As to the amusements for the evening, one of the most obvious is a potato race. Several races may be carried on at the same time.

The social committee may prepare beforehand, using water-color paper, potatoes, onions, beets, turnips, all kinds of vegetables, the paper being cut to the proper shape, and painted on one side to represent the vegetable. If you have no artist in the society adequate to this task, use the pictures in the seed catalogues, cutting them out and pasting them on cardboard.

On the other side of these paper vegetables should be written numbers and vegetable conundrums. A cardboard vegetable with a corresponding number is to contain the answer to each vegetable conundrum. These "vegetables" are distributed, and the question and answer must find their mates. This having been accomplished, the vegetable conundrums are proposed, in the order of their numbers, and guessed by the society if possible. Here are a few vegetable conundrums taken from Mrs. Whitney's bright book, " Boys at Chequassett."

> A tailor's son planted his father, and what cam up? *Ans.* Turnips.
> Plant an hour, and what comes up? *Ans.* Thyme.
> Plant tight shoes, and what comes up? *Ans.* Corn.
> Plant a French revolution, and what comes up? *Ans.* A crown imperial.
> Plant China, and what comes up? *Ans.* Beet.
> Plant auburn hair, and what comes up? *Ans.* Radish.
> Plant a dancing school, and what comes up? *Ans.* Hops.
> Plant the middle of the afternoon? *Ans.* Four o'clock.
> Plant the rising sun? *Ans.* Morning-glory.
> Plant a cat's tail? *Ans.* Fir.
> Plant a hat that has been sat upon? *Ans.* Squash.

These conundrums are simply samples; others may easily be devised.

After the conundrums may come a short entertainment devoted to vegetables. Let the song, " There was once a rosy apple," be sung, and then shown in shadow pantomime. Let some one read that famous poem of Longfellow's youth, " Mr. Finney's Turnip." There may be a reading, illustrated by moving tableaux, of Lowell's, " The Courtin'," which, it will be remembered, has to do with apple-paring. Harvest songs are abundant, and any of them will be appropriate. At the close of the evening the missionary committee will invite the society to see, spread out upon the tables, the vegetables and canned goods they have contributed. Of course the cardboard vegetables will be carried home as souvenirs.

AN ART GALLERY.

THIS form of amusement is very well known, and some of the common catches have become classic; yet it is always sure to create amusement, and if your social committee has not got up an art gallery, by all means do so.

You should curtain off a small portion of your room, and arrange the different pictures upon tables stretched along the side. Each picture is to be labelled with its title, or, if you wish, you may have a catalogue pasted in some prominent place. A small admission fee may be charged, or not. It will add to the fun if some comical genius acts as exhibitor.

Here is the best list of "works" for such an art gallery I have ever seen.

ART GALLERY.
Exhibition of Painting and Sculpture, with Many Curious Works of Art.

1. The Holy See . . . . Leo XIII.
2. Rock of Ages . . . . Lull Abi
3. Old Ironsides . . . . Bach Acre
4. The Kids at Rest . . . . Alexandre
5. Voices of the Night . . . . Thos. Katt
6. Mustered In and Mustered Out . . . . . Keene
7. A Young Man's Fear . . . . Disputed
8. Time on the Wing . . . . McGrew
9. My Own, My Native Land . . . . Anonymous

10.	Something to Adore	McHannick
11.	Can't be Beat	Annie Fool
12.	Only a Poor Old Wood-Chopper,	Geo. Washington
13.	A Perfect Foot	N. E. Carpenter
14.	Maid of Orleans	S. Orghum
15.	One Hundred Years Ago	Al. Manac
16.	Cause of the Revolution	Ole Bull
17.	Little Fishes (a study in oil)	S. R. Dean
18.	Wood Cuts (a group)	F. K. Hackman
19.	"We Part To Meet Again"	C. Steel
20.	Mementos of the Great	Cole
21.	The "Star in the East"	F. Leischmann
22.	A Spoony Couple	Unknown
23.	"Samson Was Great; Lo! a Greater"	N. Meig
24.	A Marble Group	Mike L. Angelo
25.	"Murphy on a Bender"	T. Wigg
26.	Bonaparte Crossing the Rhine	German Valley
27.	View of the Red Sea and Plains Beyond	Fairo
28.	The Skeleton Behind the Door	Unknown
29.	Deer Slayers	C. Orset
30.	Horse Fair of '96	G. Rain
31.	A Hard Case	O. Shell
32.	Heads (statuary)	C. Abbage
33.	A Wayworn Traveller	Shuman
34.	Sweet Sixteen	C. Andy
35.	"A Perfect Match"	M. Atch
36.	Hogg's Tales (illustrated)	C. Pork
37.	The Light of Other Days	T. Chandler
38.	All Afloat	S. Aylor
39.	The Ruins in China	S. M. Asher
40.	Lone Beat (an army scene)	Thtulow
41.	The Skipper's Home	O. Mite
42.	The Four Seasons	Bill
43.	Not To Be Bored	G. Imblet
44.	Noted English Essayist	Unknown
45.	The American Commentators	P. Patch

SOCIALS AND GAMES. 63

46. Whaling Implements . . . . Birch
47. Hamlet Alone . . . . H. Meat
48. Wax Figures . . . . Mrs. Jarley
49. Lay of the Last Minstrel . . . . . . B. Antem
50. Things That End in Smoke . . . . . T. Bacco
51. Crossing the Styx . . . . Sharp
52. The Lost Heir . . . . Shampooer
53. Bust of a Boy . . . . O. Close
54. The Best Thing Out . . . . M. D.
55. The Skilful Phrenologist . . . . . . M. Comb
56. A Tearful Subject . . . . G. Rocer
57. Manufacturer of New England Hoes . . K. Nitter
58. Tales of Ocean . . . . S. McArel
59. Bad Spell of Weather . . . . Unknown
60. A Friend That Sticketh Closer Than a Brother,
 McCandy
61. An Old Man's Darling and a Young Man's Slave,
 J. Smoker
62. Bridal Scene . . . . Harness
63. The Sun That Never Sets . . . . . . Shanghai
64. The Old Snuff-Taker . . . . Unknown
65. Flats and Sharps . . . . Mozart
66. Sold Again . . . . Anonymous
67. The Devil in Disguise (statuary in glass), O. Toper
68. Ever of Thee I am Fondly Dreaming . . Ban. Kerr

"The most admirable display of original specimens of art to be found in America." — *The North American Review.*

"A collection of rare and beautiful gems in the school of art, at sight of which the unbidden tears will start." — *Paris Gazette des Beaux Arts.*

"A few moments spent in its classic realms has a tendency to elevate one to higher motives." — *Atlantic Monthly.*

1. A large letter C, full of holes.
2. A cradle.
3. Flatirons.

4. Several pairs of kid gloves.
5. Two cats in a cage.
6. *Mustard* in and *mustard* out (of a bottle).
7. A mitten.
8. Watch on a turkey's wing.
9. A pan of dirt.
10. A lock and key.
11. Turnip.
12. An axe.
13. A foot-rule.
14. Molasses candy.
15. The date, 1796.
16. Tacks on tea (tax on tea).
17. A can of sardines.
18. Chips from the sawmill.
19. Scissors.
20. Coals from the grate.
21. A star in some yeast.
22. Two spoons.
23. A nutmeg-grater.
24. A group of marbles.
25. Potato on a twig that would bend.
26. Bones apart over a rind.
27. A red letter C, and carpenter's planes beyond.
28. A hoopskirt behind the door.
29. Corset.
30. Corn (horse fare).
31. Shells.
32. Cabbage.
33. An old, worn-out shoe.
34. Sixteen sticks of candy.
35. A match.
36. Hogs' tails (three or four).
37. Candles.
38. An awl in a pan of water.
39. Broken dishes.

SOCIALS AND GAMES.

40. A beet.
41. Cheese.
42. Salt, pepper, vinegar, mustard.
43. Gimlet.
44. Bacon.
45. Potatoes.
46. A bundle of switches.
47. Ham let alone.
48. Figures of sealing-wax.
49. Egg.
50. Cigars.
51. Several sticks crossed.
52. Several hairs in some butter.
53. A pair of pants stuffed, out at the knees.
54. A tooth.
55. A fine comb.
56. Onions.
57. Knitting-needles.
58. Mackerel tails.
59. "Wethair."
60. Molasses.
61. Pipe.
62. Bridle.
63. Rooster.
64. Snuffers.
65. Needles and flatirons.
66. An old shoe half-soled.
67. Bottle of whiskey.
68. Money.

A HEART PARTY.

THIS form of social will be appropriate to St. Valentine's Day. Make a large red heart of flannel and pin it upon a sheet hung from a door. In the centre of the heart sew a small circle of white. Give to each one present an arrow made of white cloth, and also a pin. Each arrow is to be numbered, corresponding numbers being given to the guests.

The members of the company are to be blindfolded in turn, and are to be led up to the sheet, upon which they pin their arrows as near as possible to the centre of the heart. Prizes are to be given to the one that comes nearest to the bull's eye, and the one that comes farthest from it. Appropriate prizes would be a heart-shaped pincushion, a heart-shaped photograph frame or pin, or a box of bonbons. For the booby prize, an appropriate symbol would be a Brownie holding a tiny heart, with an arrow inscribed " Try, try again," or a pincushion made of red satin shaped like a *beet*.

COMMERCE.

THIS is a bit of nonsense that may serve to break the ice at the opening of a social.

Each player is given ten beans and seven pieces of pasteboard upon which numbers are written, these numbers ranging from one to three hundred, if the company is large. Three minutes are given for trading, that is, for exchanging several beans for a certain number, the game being to get the most beans or the number one thinks will be the fortunate one.

At the end of this time, the leader calls for number 5, and all multiples of that, of course it being the leader's option what numbers he shall call in. Three minutes more trading are allowed, and then the leader may call in all numbers containing the figure seven, no multiples this time. The game proceeds in this way until only one number is left. The names of the holder of this and of the one that has the most beans are announced.

The social committee will, of course, have to arrange beforehand the numbers to be called in, and it will take some one of a mathematical mind so to arrange it that only one number will be left.

OLD-FASHIONED SPELLING-MATCHES.

MANY of our societies may like to hold old-fashioned spelling-matches, but these diversions are so very old-fashioned that there are not a few societies, as I know from my correspondence, that do not understand how such a match was conducted, and so I am sure the following directions will be found useful.

A good speller should be chosen to give out the words, for the reason that only a good speller will understand what words present the greatest and what the least difficulty. He should, of course, be one familiar with the dictionary, and he should provide himself beforehand with a list of especially puzzling words, to be used when he wishes to seal the fate of long-standing contestants.

He calls the meeting to order, appoints his leaders, and these, standing up, take turns in calling to their side first one and then another, until all who desire to spell have been called out. Only two sides should spell at once. If you try to carry on two spelling-matches, the audience will be confused. If more wish to spell than can be accommodated at one game, they should be divided into two parts, one spelling first, the other division second, and the victorious in each contest spelling against each other.

The sides being ranged opposite each other, the leader gives out words, alternating between the sides. When one player misses the correct spelling, he sits down, and the player opposite him is given an opportunity to try the same, and so the game proceeds until only one is left standing.

Pronouncing-matches are carried on in the same way, except that the leader spells the words, while the players pronounce. Rhyming-matches are carried on after the following fashion: the leader, who should be apt at rhyming, of course, repeats a line of poetry, making it up. Within a certain length of time the first player must complete the couplet with a line of similar length, rhyming with the leader's. If he fails, the opposite side is given an opportunity; and so it goes, like a spelling-match.

WEIGHTS AND AGES.

ARRANGE in a row the young women, and the young men in a row fronting them, having, if possible, an equal number on each side, unless some young man takes the place of a young woman, or *vice versa*.

Each young man must now write upon his card first his own age; second, his guess as to the correct weight of the young woman who faces him; and third, his estimate of the combined weight of all the young women on the opposite side. Each young woman must write on her slip her guess as to the age of the young man facing her, her own weight, and her estimate of the combined age of the opposite side. Five minutes are given in which to make the guesses.

The slips are then taken up, two or more persons being selected for this purpose. These tellers find the sum of the ages and of the weights, and of the guesses as to each. The side which wins is the one whose guesses, added together, approach most nearly the truth. The young man who guesses the nearest the combined ages of the young women, and the young woman who guesses most nearly the combined weights of the other side, also receive honorable mention, while those whose guesses are farthest removed from the truth may also be named, together with the estimates.

AN INTRODUCTION SOCIAL.

LET each member of the society wear a printed badge giving his name, and his office or committee in the society, if he has one. In a similar way adorn the visitors with badges on which their names are written in large letters. Seek to have present at the social as many of these visitors as possible, sending them special invitations. After an informal chat, let the secretary call the roll of the society, beginning with the president and the rest of the officers, and passing on to the committees and the other members.

As each name is called, let the Endeavorer who owns it take his place in a row stretching along one side of the room. Thus the society as a whole will be brought face to face with the other persons present that are not members, and the pastor in a few words introduces this body to all the others, and adds an earnest invitation to all present to join the society. He closes with an urging to mutual acquaintance, saying that no introduction will be considered necessary, as the badges will tell the names of all. The result of such a social will be quite likely to be new recruits for the society.

A STATISTICAL SOCIAL.

GIVE each person that attends the social a card containing ten printed questions with spaces for answers, and a lead pencil. Set a certain time during which these questions are to be answered. Promptly at the expiration of the time, gather the cards and hand them to the committee for examination. While this committee is preparing its report, either hold a musical and literary entertainment, or serve refreshments. Here is a sample card; the italics show the way the card was filled at one social where the plan was tried.

Young People's Society of Christian Endeavor.

FIRST CONGREGATIONAL CHURCH, AMHERST.

STATISTICS SOCIAL.

Please prepare answers to the following questions. The results of the voting, together with the most noteworthy answers, will be announced later in the evening.

1. Who is your favorite author?
   Papa, when he writes the checks.
2. At what historical event would you most like to have been present?
   When my father proposed to my mother.
3. What is your favorite flower?
   Cauliflower.
4. What do you consider the height of felicity?
   To be asleep, and yet be aware of it.
5. What is the most unfortunate position in which you could be placed?
   On my head.
6. Do you esteem married life preferable to single life, and why?
   Yes, because there is twice as much of it.
7. What character or person of every-day life could the world dispense with most advantageously?
   The chaperon.
8. What is your favorite tune?
   The tune my mother's slipper used to play.
9. Whom do you think to be the most sensible man that ever lived?
   The man who agrees with me.
10. Would you change your sex if you could, and why? Indicate present sex by writing "male" or "female" after your answer.
    Male. No, because I should be changing a certainty for an uncertainty.

On questions 1, 3, 6, 8, and 10 the statistics are to be summed up. In the social referred to, Longfellow was found to be the favorite author; sunflower the favorite flower, with "Fillsbury's best" a close second; married life decidedly preferable to single life; Yankee Doodle, the favorite tune; and far more young women dissatisfied with their sex than young men. The committee, while examining the papers for these statistics, noted the funniest answers and read them to the company. After the report of the committee, the cards that have been filled out are to be distributed among the Endeavorers, and carried home as pleasant souvenirs. Of course some time will be occupied by each Endeavorer in seeking to discover who wrote the card given him.

A BABY SOCIAL.

COVER the walls with pictures of the members of the society in their baby days. These are to be numbered, and the members, furnished with slips of paper bearing the numbers along the edge, are to guess at the identity of the various pictures, handing in their lists. The best guesser will receive honorable mention. A vote (by ballot!) may also be taken as to which member was the prettiest baby, which the most amusing, and which the ugliest!

A TENNIS SOCIAL.

STRING a tennis net firmly along a large room, with space, of course, at the ends, where the members may pass. Cut a hundred pieces of cardboard in the shape of little racquets about three inches long, and number them from one up to a hundred. Pin upon the guests small tags numbered in the same way, giving the young women the even, and the young men the odd, as far as possible. The cardboard racquets will previously have been fastened together with strings about thirty feet long, an odd racquet at one end, and an even racquet at the other, and the string intertwined among the meshes of the tennis net. Fifty of these strings will, of course, be needed.

At a given signal all the guests start to find racquets numbered to correspond with their tags, and will then proceed to disentangle the string. The couple whose racquets are first untangled will be accorded the palm. It may safely be announced at the beginning that every contestant will find a prize at the end of his string!

A NOVEL CONVERSATION SOCIAL.

A NOVEL form of conversation social may thus be arranged. As the guests enter, give each a card on which is written the topics of five-minute conversations that are to be begun at the tapping of a bell. All the cards will be numbered differently. Following each topic on every paper will be a number corresponding to the number of the card with whose owner that conversation is to be held.

The master of ceremonies will announce as the law for the evening that no one, during any five minutes of the evening, *is to speak to any one* except the person designated for that five minutes upon his card. In case he does so, a forfeit is to be collected by the social committee, to be redeemed at the close of the evening. The discovery of the person who alone can unbar the doors of speech must be made, of course, by pantomime.

MISSIONARY BOOK SOCIAL.

THIS social should not be confined to the membership of the Endeavor society, but the entire church should be invited. Urge every one who comes to bring a good missionary book, or, in lieu of that, the money to buy one. These books will furnish the nucleus of a Christian Endeavor missionary library, or they may go to the Sunday school. The entertainment of the evening should be arranged along missionary lines. Endeavorers dressed in the costumes of various missionary lands may give recitations and talks regarding those countries. Songs may be sung in various languages. Curiosities may be obtained from the different mission fields, furnishing a booth for each country, and from these booths may be served the various eatables of these foreign lands.

STRANGERS' SOCIALS.

AT a time when there seem to be a large number of strangers present in the neighborhood, hold a social especially for their benefit. In some way or other, try to introduce all of the society to all the strangers. At any rate, make them feel thoroughly at home, and seek to interest them in the society and in the church. In this way you may gain some new members, and your society will be greatly benefited simply by making the endeavor.

A QUOTATION SOCIAL.

IN announcing the social ask the members, each of them, to commit to memory beforehand three quotations. The company having gathered with these quotations, they repeat them in order, and the members are bidden to name the authors of the quotations. The first who gives correctly the author of any quotation repeated should receive a favor, either a flower, or a bright-colored ribbon that can be tied in the button-hole. At the close, the one who is most abundantly decorated will be considered the hero of the evening.

QUESTIONS AND ANSWERS.

THIS social requires some preliminary work on the part of the social committee. They must prepare a lot of questions on slips of paper, and on another set of slips a set of answers, the latter being written with no regard to the former; both questions and answers must be as different as possible. Arrange the company in two long lines facing each other. Give to the members on one side the questions and to those on the other side the answers, distributing them at random.

At a given signal the two at the head of the lines will step forward, shake hands, and say, "Good-morning." The one who holds the question will ask it, and the one who holds the answer will then repeat that. This must be repeated three times without the ghost of a smile. To laugh when asking or answering a question will send one to the foot.

A HARVEST SOCIAL.

THE society will have no difficulty in getting up this social. The room should be decorated with autumn leaves, corn-stalks, sheaves of wheat and other grains, great heaps of squashes, pumpkins, and the like. There are many pretty songs connected with harvest; such a poem as Whittier's "Mabel Martin" might be read, and illustrated by tableaux or by shadow pictures. A feature of the evening may be the requirement of certain quantities of fruit or vegetables for the admission fee, and these might be given to the poor people of the neighborhood.

Here is a capital programme for a harvest evening, arranged by Alice May Douglas: —

Instrumental Music.
Recitation: "The Last Rose of Summer." Moore.
Singing.
Original Essay: "Harvest Time and Customs."
Recitation: "The Death of the Flowers." Bryant.
Recitation: "Farewell to the Flowers." Mrs. Sigourney
Singing.
Original Essay: "Indian Summer."
Recitation: "Autumn Flowers." Caroline Southey.
Instrumental Music.
Declamation. (Subject optional.)
Singing.
Recitation: "October." Bryant.
Reading: "The Huskers." Whittier.
Singing.
Recitation: "The Child and the Autumn Leaf." Lover.
Debate: "Which is the Pleasanter Season of the Year, Summer, or Autumn?"

A RAINBOW FÊTE.

THE point of this social consists entirely in the decorations, and games of any kind may be added. The room in which the social is to be held should be decorated with all the colors of the rainbow. Lunch should be served at the small tables, each table being decorated in one of the seven rainbow colors. Flowers of corresponding colors should be placed on the tables. The shades on the lamps, the napkins and the like, as well as the caps and aprons of the waitresses, should all correspond to the color of the table.

SOCIAL GROUPS.

A SPLENDID way to promote sociability in the Christian Endeavor society is to divide the society into social groups of say ten each. The object is for the members of these groups to spend an informal evening together at least once a quarter, the groups being formed anew each quarter. The purpose kept in view is to bring together those that do not ordinarily associate with one another. Names of new members might be placed the first quarter in more than one group, so that they may the more quickly become acquainted with their co-laborers. The pastor and his wife should be invited to meet with all of the groups they can. The gathering may be held in a private house, but the entertainment should be provided by the social committee, and those whom they may summon to their assistance.

RECIPROCAL.

A PLEASANT feature of a Christian Endeavor social would be the plan of setting the young men to writing jingles on some bird and the young women to writing little poems on some flower. One Baptist society I heard of varied this amusement by asking the young women to write on the young men, and *vice versa*. These jingles are all thrown into a heap, and a good reader appointed to read them, one among the young men to read those of the young women, and a young lady to read those written by the opposite sex. After each is read there may be guesses as to its authorship, and the company may, on the conclusion of the whole, vote as to which is the best.

SONGS IN PICTURES.

GIVE each member of the company a slip of paper on which has been written the title of some well-known song, furnishing him also with pencil and a piece of drawing paper. The task set before him is to illustrate on the drawing paper the song whose name has been given him. Of course only the most familiar songs should be chosen. The slip of paper contains a number, and the drawing is to be numbered to correspond. When all have finished this artistic work, the drawings are to be fastened by pins upon a string tightly stretched across one end of the room at a height convenient to be seen.

Next, every member of the company receives a slip of paper bearing upon its left edge a column of figures corresponding to the numbers upon the slips originally distributed, and the Endeavorers are required to move along the line of drawings, writing upon the paper the names of the songs intended to be illustrated, so far as they can guess them. These papers when completed are handed in to the social committee, who examines them, and honors in some appropriate way the best as well as the worst of the guessers.

A QUEER COURT.

ALL societies by this time are familiar with the plan of having their members each try to earn a dollar by a certain time, and then tell at a social how the dollar has been earned. A pleasing variety of this plan is to have the society on the appointed evening resolve itself into a court. The chairman of the social committee may act as district attorney, and the pastor as the judge. Divide the members that have earned their dollar into two companies. Require the members of the first company to set before the society, in plain or elaborate fashion, as they desire, how their dollars have been earned. A jury previously appointed retires after the close of the recitals, and comes back bringing a verdict declaring which one of the members earned the dollar in the best way. In the same way the remaining division are tried, and one found similarly "guilty."

Next these two "guilty" ones are required to choose, each of them, a lawyer from among the young men. These lawyers have to plead their cases, each trying to prove that his client has earned the dollar in the best way. At the close of the pleas the judge charges the jury, which retires to find a verdict for one of the two. The one who is found "guilty" is sentenced to accept a handsome little present from the social committee for his earnest endeavors.

It adds a little fun, if the society is well balanced as to sex, to make up the first company entirely of young women, and the second entirely of young men. The young woman found "guilty" is compelled to choose a lawyer from the opposite sex, and *vice versa*. It only remains to say that the company of Endeavorers is to sing hymns while the jury is out.

AN EVENING IN GREENLAND.

DECORATE the room in which the social is held with paper icicles. All the decorations, and the costumes of the social committee, should remind one of ice and snow. Ices will make appropriate refreshments. Papers and talks should be given discussing the country, and the habits of the people. Poems on Jack Frost, snow, and similar frigid subjects may be recited, and songs concerning cold weather, sleighing, and the like, may be sung. Of course, such a social as this is most fittingly held in midsummer.

A NUT SOCIAL.

THE feature of the evening that gives its name to the social is the following puzzle. Copies of it, made on a manifolder, are to be handed about, and given to each person in the room.

Nuts to Crack.

1. Lazhe
2. Pance
3. Hlabselkr
4. Madlon
5. Ecbeh
6. Hogtundu
7. Chykoir
8. Noarc
9. Buntruett
10. Briftel
11. Hunttecs
12. Metung
13. Uawltn
14. Tuocanoc

Name
Number

At the end of a certain time, the player who has most successfully solved the fourteen anagrams, each hiding the name of some nut, is accounted the victor. Appropriate refreshments at the close of this test will be raisins and well-cracked nuts, neatly tied up in Japanese napkins. Under the heading of "Nuts to Crack," in "Social Evenings," are described further amusements appropriate to this social.

CLASS RECEPTIONS.

THE social committee of a large society will do a good thing if occasionally it singles out different classes of the members, and holds receptions for them. For example, the associate members may be given a reception, to which the lookout committee alone may be invited, in addition to the associates. Another reception may be given in honor of the honorary members. Another reception may be given to the older young people that are not members. The older society may give a reception to the Juniors, or to the primary class of the Sunday school, and the like. Some social may be distinguished by the presence, on special invitation, of all the church officers.

ORANGE SOCIALS.

DECORATE the room with white and yellow cheesecloth, and with orange-colored tissue paper, worked in fantastic shapes. Deck small tables with white tissue paper and amber glass. The orange tissue paper will appear here also, in the form of napkins prettily arranged. The waiters will wear orange-colored aprons and dainty orange caps. The refreshments will consist of oranges and sponge-cake, while the entertainment of the evening will be made up of talks by those who have visited the South and other orange-growing countries, and who will tell about the fruit and its surroundings. Attractive music will add to the festivities.

A HIT-OR-MISS SOCIAL.

To arouse curiosity, send out invitations to this social, calling it a "hit-or-miss social," and placing in the corner confused dashes of different colored paints. Various hit-or-miss games will make up the amusement of the evening. The first is "hit-or-miss questions and answers," briefly described in "Social Evenings." Two boxes are provided, with holes in the covers through which hands can be thrust, drawing forth all kinds of odd-shaped bits of paper, — stars, circles, triangles, ovals, etc. Each piece of paper bears a word.

The Endeavorers are furnished with pencils, and instructed to write on their bits of paper two questions about the object named thereon. On the other side of the paper, without mentioning the name of the object, each is to write two remarks regarding it. The questions may contain the name of the object, but it should be especially announced that this name must not appear in the remarks.

After this has been accomplished, the players are instructed to hunt out, each of them, a player with the same shaped paper (there being two papers of each shape). Then, the company being quieted, one player of each couple reads the questions he has written, and the other player answers each question with one of the remarks he has written. Of course, the questions and remarks being upon different subjects, the result will be extremely amusing. In the case of one evening where this game was tried, as described in *The Youth's Companion*, one girl, holding one of these matched cards, inquired if her partner did not love pansies. His reply was that they were savage creatures, and that he had once seen one which had killed a man. Then in his turn he asked his partner questions on panthers, and she declared that she kept them in every room of the house all summer; her mother raised splendid great ones in the garden. One young man whose remarks were upon needle-work was questioned upon the Battle of Gettysburg, and asserted that it was "well enough for girls," but "as for me, give me something more stirring."

A "hit-or-miss conversation" is next in order. Each member of the company draws from a box a slip of paper which will bear a number and a subject for conversation. Six or seven of these slips will bear the same number and the same topic, and thus the room will be divided into groups discussing different subjects.

"Hit-or-miss characters" affords a third amusement. A large sheet of cardboard is pinned against the wall, and upon it are fastened what seem to be immense autumn leaves, gorgeously painted. The members are blind-folded, one after the other, and marched up to the cardboard. Thrusting out a hand, each places it on one of these leaves, which becomes the property of the player. Upon the back of it is written a character, and the player reads aloud the description of himself thus drawn.

As the guests leave the room, each takes from a basket a "hit-or-miss souvenir." These consist of bright paper, prettily cut and folded, and tied with baby ribbon. On the inside are written mottoes and good wishes.

INTRODUCTIONS.

A PLEASANT feature of a Christian Endeavor social where many strangers are present will be the forming of two long lines which are introduced to one another, and after this thorough fashion: The two at the head of the column start and shake hands all down through the rows, introducing themselves to every one else in the room; and they are followed by the others in turn.

MISSIONARY GAMES.

OUR societies are so greatly interested in missions, and already have so much missionary information, that games based upon this knowledge may be undertaken without fear of failure. For example, "countries and characters" may be played, after the fashion of the familiar game of "beast, bird and fish" described in "Social Evenings." One player throws a knotted handkerchief to another and calls out, "Africa," "China," "India," or some other mission land, then counts ten, if possible, before the second player can name some worker or some place connected with the country specified.

Another game is to decide upon some letter, and then have a contest to see what Endeavorer in the room can in a certain time write the longest list of names of places or persons, in mission countries, beginning with that letter.

The familiar "geography game" can be played upon a missionary basis, the company being arranged in two groups, a letter being taken, and each group shouting to the other in turn the name of some town or other geographical feature, in mission lands, beginning with the required letter. As each group shouts out its name, the other group must reply before the leader can count ten deliberately. In case of failure, one player is chosen from the group that has failed, and passes over to the other side, and after a new letter is fixed upon the game proceeds until one side is entirely annihilated.

GERMAN SOCIALS.

THE German social is, in every particular, like the better-known Scotch social. If lunch is served, the waiters are dressed as Germans. The guests, as they enter, are to be received by young maidens and old ladies dressed in German attire, and using German phrases with as great freedom as they can.

The programme of the evening consists of recitations and songs in the German language, together with talks or essays about great Germans, and recitations of some German poems translated into English. Pictures of German authors and composers may adorn the walls. The instrumental music should also be by Germans. The refreshments that are served should partake as largely as possible of the same national flavor.

IT RESTS.

THIS is a clever catch that would serve to enliven a Christian Endeavor social, filling in the space between more dignified games. To accomplish the trick it is necessary that two of the players know the secret and work together. One of these may leave the room, but before he does so both the confederates should notice who is the last person to speak. The door being closed, the inside player puts his hand on some one's head and cries out, "It rests." This he does with a second person, and again with a third, selecting this time the person who spoke last before the confederate withdrew, and cries out, "On whom does it rest?" To the astonishment of the company, the person in the other room will at once name the Endeavorer thus selected. The performance can be repeated many times before the company will guess how it is carried on.

STEAMBOAT'S COMING!

To play this lively and profitable game, let the company be seated in a circle. A handkerchief is knotted into a loose ball that can be thrown effectively.

Some one takes this ball and throws it at any one he chooses, saying, "Steamboat's coming! What's it loaded with?" The person who is hit must at once reply with the name of an article not already given in the course of the game, and beginning with a certain letter previously determined on. In case he fails before ten is counted by the one who threw the ball, he pays a forfeit.

This game is quite a brisk one, as the thrower may indulge in as many feints as he chooses before he throws the ball, and the counting of the ten will serve as quite a perplexing source of confusion.

PROGRESSIVE GAMES.

WHERE the society meets in a Sunday-school room built after the modern style with classrooms opening on the sides of the room, this social may be arranged with little trouble. It is easily carried on where the social is held in a private house. If only one room is at the disposal of the social committee, it should be partitioned off with shawls and sheets into, say, five smaller rooms.

As the members enter, each is decorated with a card which reads, "Room 1," or "Room 2," or "3," or "4," or "5." Each of these cards admits the member bearing it into one of the rooms, the rooms being numbered; and here he finds some one who directs those assembled in the playing of some special game. At the tap of a bell, all the Endeavorers pass to the room immediately above them in the order of number, and play the games that hold sway in those rooms. Of course the social committee will so plan the games as to have a pleasing variety, and will place in superintendence of each room one perfectly familiar with the game to be played there during the evening. In this way the Endeavorers pass around the circle, until it comes time for refreshments.

A SCRIPTURE AUTOGRAPH SOCIAL.

EVERY one present is to be presented with a small blank book in which he is to get the other members of the company to write Scripture quotations. Each m ist sign his name to the quotation he gives. After the books are well filled, call for quiet and bid the Endeavorers read, in turn, the quotations that have been given them, calling for the names of the books of the Bible from which the quotations are taken. Let the secretary keep account, and announce, after all are through, who has been the first to name correctly the largest number of books.

MIND-READING.

IN " Social Evenings," there are given a variety of methods of carrying on the amusing catch called " mind-reading," but here is an exceedingly puzzling method not named in that book. Ask each of those who are to engage in the game to write upon a slip of paper the name of something. Put all these names in a box, and let the mind-reader draw from it the slips, rubbing each slip against his forehead, and, after a pretended rumination, naming what is written.

The first time he names the object he himself wrote, opens the paper as if for confirmation, and reads, of course, not what he, but what some one else wrote. With the second slip he names this object, proceeding thus until the last. Of course all in the room will agree that he has named precisely what they wrote, and it will be long before they guess how the feat was accomplished. The reader must take care to select last of all the slip he himself wrote, and the slips must be nearly enough alike, and folded in so uniform a way, that no one will recognize his own slip.

SHIP SOCIAL TICKETS.

IN "Social Evenings," I have described quite thoroughly a ship social. Some Endeavorers have got up attractive tickets which harmonize with this form of social, and many societies will like to use one of the two following:

TRANSFERABLE.

No. 1822 B.

FIRST PRESBYTERIAN STEAMSHIP CO.

CABIN.

M ....

STEAMER
GOLDEN GATE.

Promise Fairweather, Captain.

Voyage, Thursday, September 27,
8 P.M.

CONDITIONS.

In the event of the loss or detention of the ship, during the voyage, by any of the accidents of navigation or dangers of the sea, no liability of any kind shall attach to company; neither shall said company be under any obligation to forward passengers to their respective homes at close of voyage; neither shall they be responsible for any seasickness, nor refund the amount of passage.

SOCIALS AND GAMES. 91

Baggage, other than the regulation shopping-satchel, will not be received.

The above steamer, *Golden Gate*, will receive passengers at pier, corner Van Ness Avenue and Sacramento Street, on THURSDAY EVENING, at 8 o'clock.

Good for THIS VOYAGE ONLY.
Fare, 25 cents.

THOMAS CHINK,   ERNEST SHIPMAN,
    Purser.   G. P. & T. A.

W. A. Y. P. S. C. E. Line.	REFRESHMENT COUPON. *Present at Steward's Cabin.*	MUSIC COUPON. *Present to W. A. Glee Club.*	PHYSICIAN'S COUPON. *If seasick*
This Ticket Entitles Holder to One First-Class Passage ON Ship *ENDEAVOR* Sails from Company's Landing, Walnut Avenue, Wednesday, Feb. 6, 1895, at 8 P.M. *Stops made at "Tête-à-tête Pier," "Point Cheerup," and "Social Town."* B. E. MERRIE, G. P. A.			

THEIR WEIGHT.

THIS contest will make pleasant material to fill some interval in your socials. Let the committee previously gather six articles as dissimilar as may be in size, shape, and material, but each weighing a pound. You may take, for instance, a wooden pail, a tin pan, a piece of lead. Call out different members of the company, and request them to arrange these six articles in the order of their weight. Of course almost every one will think the large articles to be the heaviest. Keep this up until the interest in the matter flags, or until some one guesses the truth.

POETICAL DESCRIPTIONS.

AN interesting game is based on poetical descriptions of famous persons. A large number of these are copied from well-known writers. Each is placed at the bottom of a slip of paper. The players begin at the top of the slip, and write, in turn, the names of the persons supposed to be described by the quotations, turning the paper over so as to hide what each has written from the one to whom he passes it. For example, a recent party wrestled with this from Tennyson: —

> "A thousand claims to reverence closed
> In her as mother, wife, and queen."

This, of course, referred to Queen Victoria, but one jocose player guessed that it referred to Liliuokalani. Again, another quotation was used from Lowell: —

> "The kindly, earnest, brave, foreseeing man,
> Sagacious, patient, dreading praise, not blame,
> New birth of our new soil, the first American."

This referred, of course, to Abraham Lincoln, but a few of the players got it George Washington.

Here are a few more samples: —

> "I need not praise the sweetness of his song
> Where limpid verse to limpid verse succeeds
> Smooth as our Charles."
>
> [Referring to Longfellow.]

SOCIALS AND GAMES. 93

"This laurel, greener from the brows
　Of him that uttered nothing base."
　　　　　　　　　[Tennyson on Wordsworth.]

"Westward still points the inexorable soul."
　　　　　　　　　　　　　　　[Columbus.]

"He seems to me
Scarce other than my own ideal knight,
Who reverenced his conscience as his king;
Whose glory was, redressing human wrong;
Who spoke no slander, no, nor listened to it;
Who loved one only, and who clave to her."
　　　　　　　　　　　　　[Prince Albert.]

"The man of amplest influence,
　Yet clearest of ambitious crime,
　Our greatest yet with least pretence,
　Great in council and great in war,
　Foremost captain of his time,
　Rich in saving common sense,
　And, as the greatest only are,
　In his simplicity sublime."
　　　　　　　　　　　　　[Wellington.]

". . . The first warbler, whose sweet breath
　Preluded those melodious bursts that fill
　The spacious times of great Elizabeth
　With sounds that echo still."　　[Chaucer.]

"In a small chamber, friendless and unseen,
　Toiled o'er his types one poor, unlearned young man;
　The place was dark, unfurnitured, and mean; —
　Yet there the freedom of a race began."
　　　　　　　　　　　　　　[Garrison.]

A QUEER EXAMINATION.

As the members of the society arrive let them be registered, and let each be handed by the social committee an examination paper like the following, which shows both sides. Of course, some changes will be necessary, to adapt the questions to the church and denomination.

Special . . . Announcements.	Departmental . . . Regulations.
1. You are always welcome at our **SOCIALS**.	I. All present *are* students (*pro tem*).
2. You will also be welcome at the **Prayer Meetings** held every Saturday evening at eight o'clock in the Church Parlor, *166 Windsor Street*.	II. Students *must* copy from each other.
	III. Students shall *not* answer questions on their own papers.
	IV. Students *stationary* may be expelled or fined at the discretion of the principal.
Come whenever, and with as many as, you can.	V. Medals will be awarded for:— (*a*) Greatest number of errors. (*b*) Fewest questions answered. (*c*) Last paper filed with examiners within allotted time.

EXAMINATION.
(SOCIAL.)
WINTER SESSION.

E. L. OF C. E.
Dominion Square Methodist Church, Montreal.
MARCH 22, 1895.

Name of Student, ...

SOCIALS AND GAMES. 95

SOCIAL.
DOMINION SQUARE
METHODIST CHURCH,
March 22, 1895.

EXAMINATION PAPER.
TIME, ONE HOUR.

Students may take any six of the following subjects.

EXAMINERS:
Local Society, E. L. of C. E.
REV. W. J. HUNTER, D.D., Pastor.
W. F. IRWIN, President.

No. 1. Methodism.

(*a.*) Date when people were first called Methodists?

(*b.*) In what city was organized the first Methodist society?

(*c.*) When was Methodist union in Canada consummated?

(*d.*) When will the next General Conference be held?

No. 2. Sunday School.

(*a.*) Name of founder of Sunday schools?

(*b.*) In what year was the first Sunday school organized?

(*c.*) What country has the largest number of Sunday schools?

(*d.*) What denomination in Montreal has the largest number of Sunday schools?

No. 3. Christian Endeavor.

(*a.*) In what year was Christian Endeavor started?

(*b.*) By whom was the first society organized?

(*c.*) In what city was the first society started?

(*d.*) How many societies are there in the Montreal Union?

No. 4. Epworth League.

(*a.*) In what year was the Epworth League organized?

(*b.*) In what country did the movement originate?

(*c.*) Date when the first Canadian League was formed?

(*d.*) Name of the place where the first Canadian League was started?

No. 5. Junior Endeavor.

(*a.*) How many years organized?

(*b.*) Whose idea was it originally?

(*c.*) In which Montreal denomination numerically strongest?

(*d.*) Name of church where first Montreal society started?

No. 6. This Church.

(*a.*) In what year was this church erected?

(*b.*) Name of first pastor?

(*c.*) Name of a former pastor now in the mission field?

(*d.*) What rank among the Methodist churches of Canada in missionary givings?

The regulations printed upon the examination paper are self-explanatory. Notice the requirement, "Students may take any six of the following subjects." As only six subjects are laid down, the point is obvious. A special introduction committee is to be moving constantly about among the company, introducing one to another, and helping the guests fill up their papers, when they can find no one from whom to copy.

The examination paper that each Endeavorer works upon bears the name of some other student, and for this reason each person will be especially anxious to fill up the examination paper on which he is working, in order that the other fellow may not get a medal for the greatest number of errors, or for the fewest questions answered, and, besides, each tries to hand in his paper to the examiners as early as possible, in order that the Endeavorer for whom he is working may not receive a medal for the last paper filed. Of course each Endeavorer hopes that the paper on which his own name occurs will, through the slowness or carelessness of the other members, receive one or more of these medals.

The plan is somewhat complicated, but I hope I have made it plain. The medals are made, one of wood, one of brass, and one of leather. Stamped upon each may be the words, "Exam. Social."

A QUILTING PARTY.

IF you are fortunate enough to have any old people in your church that can tell you about the old-fashioned quilting-bees, you will have great fun in carrying on one yourself. Place upon frames the comfortables ready to be tied. Require every one to tie at least ten knots. After the completion of this work, have recitations of old-fashioned poems, such as those by Will Carleton, and close with old-time refreshments, such as pop-corn, hickory nuts, molasses candy, and apples.

A HOME MISSION SOCIAL.

SOCIALS based upon foreign missions are common, but there are not many based upon home missions. To get up a good home mission social, let different members of the society agree to represent, on that evening, an Indian, an African, a Chinaman, a Mormon, a Mountain White, a Jew, a Russian, and others of the classes among whom our home missionaries work. All these are to make five-minute speeches in the characters they represent, describing their lives, and incidentally hinting that they need missionary work, and the good to be obtained from it. Appropriate songs may enliven the programme.

THROWING THE HANDKERCHIEF.

ALL the persons present are seated in a circle about the room, with the exception of the leader, who stands in the centre. A handkerchief is knotted and thrown from one member of the circle to another. The leader attempts to catch it in its rapid flight. If he succeeds, the person who threw the handkerchief must take his place in the centre, and strive in his turn to catch the flying missile.

THE KEY TO CHARACTER.

TAKE a common door-key and give it to one of the members, at the same time whispering to him, and telling him to give it to some else of the company who possesses a certain characteristic. Having made selection, this player hands it to a second player, whispering in his ear instructions that he is to hand the key to some one else in the company possessing another kind of qualification; and so the key goes around until a large number have received it.

Then each one speaks in turn, the first player saying, for example, "I gave this key to Mr. A, and told him to give it to the wittiest person in the room." Mr. A says, "I gave this key to Miss B, and told her to give it to the greatest mimic in the room." Miss B says, "I gave this key to Mr. C, and told him to give it to the person who was to become a great orator"; and so it goes. Of course, the fun lies in the appropriateness or absurdity of the choice made to fit each requirement. In a company of Endeavorers, there will, of course, be no fear that any ill-natured hits will be made, or that anything will occur to wound the feelings of any player.

OLD MAIDS' REPAIR-SHOP.

THIS is a pretty little pantomime, which may be used to introduce a social, or to fill up some interval. Thirteen old maids march in along one end of the room, their faces all wrinkled; and they are dressed in all kinds of queer ways. They grieve over their ugliness, and wring their hands in despair. Their actions may be interpreted by some Endeavorer in a bright little speech, or, if any one of the society is sufficiently skilled, a short song may be written for them to sing.

On one side of the room is a curtain, from which projects a crank. While the old maids are bemoaning their fate, the proprietor comes out and hangs up a sign reading, "Old Maids' Repair-Shop." This sign the old maids see with great rejoicing. One at a time approaches the curtain, is received by the proprietor, and ushered in. He comes out, gives a few turns to the crank, and forth steps a beautiful young girl, who walks off with great rejoicing, evidently envied by the other old maids, each of whom in turn submits to the same transformation. The last old maid so taxes the machine that it breaks with a loud noise.

HARLEQUIN.

EACH person of the company is given a tally card tied with a long string, which is double. The string is for use in the first game. A list of these games is written upon the card, which reads as follows:

1. Cat's Cradle.
2. Bean Porridge Hot.
3. Laughing.
4. Whistling.
5. Silence is golden.
6. Refreshments.
7. If not yourself, who would you rather be?

During a given time partners are obtained for each of these seven exercises, the names being written opposite the numbers. At the stroke of a bell, all begin to play cat's cradle for four or five minutes, or less, if thought best. Number 2 and number 6 explain themselves. For number 3, the members of the company must look at their partners and laugh to some familiar tune played on the piano. Number 4 is similar. For number 5 the entire company must sit in absolute silence. Number 7 is conversation on that subject.

LEMON SOCIALS.

THE social committee will add a pleasing element of mystery to the coming social, if in the announcement of it they require each Endeavorer to bring a lemon. It will afterwards be discovered that these lemons are to make lemonade. As the lemons are handed in at the door, let the committee take charge of them, and cut them open. Require each Endeavorer present to squeeze his own lemon, lemon-squeezers being provided, and to count the number of seeds therein. Distinguish in some way those whose lemons contain the smallest and the largest number of seeds.

After the lemons have been squeezed, the seeds, being carefully separated, should be placed in a bottle, and the Endeavorers should be asked to guess how many seeds are in the bottle. A suitable reward should be given the one who guesses nearest the truth, and a booby prize may distinguish the poorest guesser. These prizes should be presented with comic speeches.

BIRTHDAY SOCIALS.

THE following invitation to a birthday social will describe pretty well the plan of the gathering. With these invitations each Endeavorer is to receive a pretty little bag of brightly colored silk, in which he is expected to place as many pennies as he is years old.

Y. P. S. C. E. Birthday Social.

At the residence of W. H. PUTNAM, Monday Evening,
February 4, 1895.

This birthday party
  Is given to you;
We hope you will come,
  And promise, if you do,
An agreeable time,
  Some good things to eat,
And, besides many others,
  A musical treat.
As we could not secure
  The number of candles,
To let your light shine,
  We send this fandangle.
Put safely within it
  As many round pennies
As years you are old;
  We hope you are many!
Your light will be bright
  If you send it or bring it,
While we keep it dark,
  If you wish, what is in it.
The social committee,
  With greetings most hearty,
Feel sure you will come
  To your own birthday party!

The entertainment for the birthday socials is to be prepared beforehand. Discover twelve members of the society whose birthdays fall in the twelve months of the year, and get these to write, or get somebody to write for them, poems upon those months, each lauding his as the best month of the twelve. Prepare also songs, one for each of the four seasons, and, if thought best, one tableau as well for each season. In giving this programme, those whose birthdays fall in the spring months will first read their poems, then will come the spring song, and the spring tableau may close the whole; and so with the other seasons. After the poem for each month has been read, those whose birthdays fall in that month will go forward and solemnly present their bags of pennies. You may close with a debate as to the best season in which to have one's birthday!

A WISHBONE SOCIAL.

The society that originated this social provided, painted upon pasteboard, the heads and upper portions of the bodies of two women and two men. These were placed on the platform back of a low curtain, and so hung that one at a time could be raised in view, or all together. The first part of the programme was a quartette in which these four comical figures took part, one jerking up and singing a solo, on the conclusion of which the other three added their voices for the chorus. The song, which was devised by an ingenious Endeavorer, was to the tune of "The bullfrog on the bank," and was a wishbone song, starting with the following verse: —

"O I wish I owned the moon
And could use it as I please,
I'd cut it up in little bits
And feed the world with cheese,"

the chorus joining in with,

"Singing tra la la la la la la la la, *etc.*
A wish upon a wishbone, at a wishbone social too."

It will be necessary to provide an encore for the quartette!

In order to match up for the refreshments, each young man was given a card upon which was written the name of some person, and each young woman another card on which was written the name of something that person especially wished for; for example, Alexander, "more worlds to conquer"; Richard III., "a horse"; Columbus, "India"; Sir John Franklin, "the northwest passage"; Little Jack Horner, "a plum"; Humpty Dumpty, "to get up again." Each young man having found what he wished for, there is still another ceremony to be accomplished before the refreshment tables are reached. A number of cookies cut in the shape of wishbones have been provided, and each couple must step to the front and wish upon these wishbones. Some comical genius attired as a phrenologist will examine the head of the successful competitor, and tell what he wished for by investigation of the bumps, explaining, in learned phrase, his characteristics to the audience. Before this loses its interest, permit the entire company to go to the refreshment tables.

A JOURNEY BY MAP.

THE missionary committee may take charge of the evening. Much work must be done beforehand. Select the route over which the society is to travel, with an eye to the missionary interest that may be excited and the missionary information that may be given. A journey among the missionary fields of your own denomination would be best.

Assign different portions of the route to different Endeavorers. One is to describe the start from New York, another the ocean voyage, a third the arrival on the first mission field and the scenes that there will greet the traveller, a fourth should carry the audience on to a second mission field, and so forth. Each guide will provide himself with pictures and curios and maps, — whatever will help to make his recital vivid. Opportunities for questions may be given at the end of each little speech.

EVERYTHING FROM A NUTSHELL.

SELL during the evening all kinds of nuts, whole or cracked, as well as various kinds of nut-cake, hickory-nut, walnut, almond, cocoanut, and so on. Salted almonds, drinks made from cocoa, and other eatables and drinkables, may be had, and there may be sold also various little articles made from nuts, such as thimble cases contrived from English walnuts cut in halves, gilded, neatly lined with silk, and tied together with silk cords. Acorns gilded and glued together can also be fashioned into articles of usefulness or adornment.

For the evening's entertainment cut peanuts in two, remove the kernel, and write upon tissue paper various directions for the players. Place the paper inside the halves of the shells, and tie them together. Get as many as will to accept these, promising to endeavor, at least, to accomplish the orders contained therein. One, on opening his, will find himself required to recite a comic poem; another, to sing a duet with a third; another, to impersonate Hamlet; another, to repeat the alphabet backwards, and so on.

AN INTERNATIONAL TEA.

DRAPE the room with flags and colors of the different nations, hanging upon the walls whatever will serve to remind one of foreign lands. After the guests have arrived, girls appropriately dressed to represent America, Italy, Scotland, France, England, Germany, and other lands, step one by one in front of the audience and sing the national songs of their countries, — the " Star Spangled Banner," " The Watch on the Rhine," the Marseillaise, " Scots wha ha'e wi' Wallace bled," " God save the Queen," " Beautiful Venice, the bride of the sea," and so on.

Each will carry the flag of the country she represents. On the conclusion of the songs there may be a march of the nations, in which various evolutions may be prettily carried out.

America will wear the red, white, and blue. Germany will have braids of yellow hair, a short blue skirt and black bodice, and a red waist. France may have a lavender skirt, a black velvet bodice and white waist, and a dainty white cap. The Scotch lassie will wear a short skirt and waist of plaid, with a plaid sash about the shoulder, hanging down at the side. Her cap will be of the same material. England may wear white, and be draped in the national banner. Italy may wear a green skirt, red bodice and white waist, with red and yellow handkerchief about her head, while large earrings adorn her ears.

At the conclusion of this pretty entertainment the audience may be invited to the supper room, where, for a proper fee, they will be given their choice of tables presided over by young ladies of the different nationalities. America's table will groan under such Yankee food as baked beans, brown bread, doughnuts, codfish cakes, succotash, and — of course — pie. Scotland's porridge and oat cakes will give wholesome invitation, together with cheese, scones, and haggis. Italy will preside over vermicelli soup, macaroni, spaghetti, cheese, grapes, and figs. Germany will offer sauerkraut, sausage, and pretzels. The dainty French table will present delicate rolls, delicious coffee, omelet, and a salad. On England's table will be a huge roast of beef and a plum pudding.

I have condensed in the foregoing an account by Adelaide Rouse.

QUAKER.

This old-fashioned game is so very old that it will be new to most circles. The Juniors will especially be pleased with it. The players seat themselves in a circle, and the leader, shaking his right hand vigorously up and down, turns to his neighbor with the inquiry, "Neighbor, neighbor, how art thee?" His politeness is rewarded with the reply, "I am well, as thou dost see." The leader goes on to ask, "How's the neighbor next to thee?" and the second player responds, "I don't know, but I'll go see."

As the second player proceeds with the formula, turning to the third player, he commences himself to shake his right hand vigorously up and down, and so it continues until the entire circle is set to this exercise. While the right hands are still wagging, the leader begins again with the same set of questions, at the same time shaking his left hand also. Thus it proceeds until first right and then left foot are set in motion, and finally the heads of all are wagging backward and forward, unless, indeed, long before this point is reached, laughter and fatigue have brought the game to an end.

Still another form of this game is entitled, "Home from India." The leader says, "My father is home from India." His neighbor asks, "What did he bring you?" The answer is, "A fan," the leader proceeding to fan himself with one hand. This gesture passes around the circle until it reaches the leader again, who reiterates his former remark, "My father is home from India," and when questioned,

"What did he bring you?" answers, "Two fans," both hands vigorously waving. Before the end of the game a boot and a shoe are successively added, and finally a hat, by which time both feet and the head as well as the hands are set in vigorous motion.

DOUBLETS.

This game was invented by that witty Englishman, Lewis Carroll, one of whose problems was this: Change "head" to "tail" in five moves. With each move one letter of the original word may be dropped, and another letter substituted in the same place to make a new word, the successive moves culminating in the word "tail." For example: —

> head,
> heal,
> teal,
> tell,
> tall,
> tail.

You may divide the company into sets, and propose some such doublet as that for their solution, the side first solving it having the privilege of drawing one player from the opposite side, the process continuing until one side or the other loses heart or all of its players. A similar game may be based on any sort of word puzzle.

A WEEK IN A DAY.

This is a dainty plan for an evening's entertainment, and will afford at the same time pleasure and some money return, with slight outlay.

Partition the room in which the social is to be held into compartments sacred to the various days of the week. Sell in the division devoted to Monday articles pertaining to washday, such as aprons, clothes-pin bags, baby washtubs, and the like. Your grocer may have some new kind of soap that he would like to introduce, and a practical young woman, prettily dressed, may give a working illustration of its virtues.

Tuesday's booth will contain the articles suitable for ironing day; Wednesday's, everything for mending day. Thursday is reception day, and that apartment will be nicely arranged as a parlor, in which tea, cake, and other edibles will be served. Friday is sweeping day, and in that division will be stored for sale all sorts of brushes and brooms, dust-bags, dust-caps, and so on. Saturday is baking day, and its division may contain a little bakery in operation, the products of which, as well as of many a home bakery, will be offered to customers.

For Sunday, organize an old-fashioned choir, dressed in garb of the olden time, and at a certain point in the evening let them march in from an anteroom and sing the old-time airs for a suitable conclusion to the evening.

A JAPANESE SOCIAL.

HANG the walls of the room with Japanese flags, wall-rolls, and pictures and curios of all kinds. A diligent search among the families of almost any town will be rewarded by the discovery of a large number of very entertaining curios. One of the first exercises after the entrance of the guests may be the conveying of a party of Cook's tourists around the room, stopping at each object of interest, which is explained by some competent guide.

Japanese screens will partition off the corners of the room, and the guests who do not choose to join the Cook's tourists may, a couple at a time, enter these miniature dwellings, and be served with tea in Japanese fashion by the master and mistress of the house, who are clothed in the attire of the country.

Between the various numbers of the evening's programme all present are required to seat themselves, Japanese fashion, upon the floor, their heels serving as sufficient chairs. This attitude will effectually keep them awake, while one who has posted himself upon the subject gives, with the aid of a map, a sketch of Japanese missions, especially indicating the places where the missionaries of the denomination to which the society belongs are doing their work. At another point of the evening some one may give an outline of the recent Japan-China war.

In a social of this kind that I lately attended, the three-hour Japanese ceremonial tea was condensed into half an hour for our edification, two daintily attired girls taking the parts of mistress and servant, while two lads in Japanese robes patiently waited for the three swallows of tea vouchsafed them after most elaborate preparations.

Early in the evening a blackboard was exhibited upon which were written the names of the important Japanese cities, and underneath each the names of

SOCIALS AND GAMES. 111

the principal missionaries of the denomination at work in each. It was announced that a certain time would be given for the study of this list, and groups were gathered around it while others were making the Cook's tour, or visiting the little Japanese houses in the corners. Toward the end of the evening the blackboard was turned with its face toward the wall, all were provided with pencils and paper, and required to duplicate the list of towns and missionaries as well as they could.

A committee received these lists, and while they were at work the company were formed in two long lines facing each other, to play a regular Japanese game. The only implements required are the hands. Advancing from their rows, the heads of the columns shake their hands vigorously from side to side three times in concert, repeating three Japanese words for which plain American, "One, two, three!" will answer. With the "three," each extends his hand toward the other. The hand is extended in one of three ways: either with the fist closed, like a stone; or with the palm flat, like a piece of paper; or with the first and second fingers extended, like a pair of scissors. If the opponents have chosen the same form, the trial must be made again; but if A has chosen the stone and B the paper, the latter is victorious, because the paper can wrap up the stone. If A has chosen the scissors and B the paper, the former is victorious, because the scissors can cut the paper. If A has chosen the scissors and B the stone, the latter is victorious, because the stone can spoil the scissors. The player who is victorious is permitted to drop out of the lines, while the one who is conquered must remain. So it goes on down the rows, opposite players contesting with one another until all have tried it. Then again the heads of the row go through the form, and so on until one row is entirely vanquished. After this game is thoroughly understood, those facing each other all down the lines may go through the operation simultaneously, thus making the game very rapid.

But by this time the committee had completed its examination, and was ready to report. To the authors of the best and the worst papers prizes were presented in Japanese fashion. The judge and the contestant having seated themselves upon the floor, to which their foreheads were touched with many profound genuflections, the judge, imitating the Japanese phrasing, said, "Most illustrious and highly exalted victor, your abased and worthless servant lifts up to you this honorable prize, in token of astonishment and admiration at your profound and most impressive learning. Will your honorable highness deign to receive this insignificant token of our profound esteem?" And then followed more genuflections.

When the time came to go home, the entertainers seated themselves, Japanese fashion, at one end of the room, and all the guests on retiring were obliged to seat themselves opposite, bowing to the floor three times to express their satisfaction at the evening's entertainment, and heartily inviting their hosts to come and see them at *their* homes.

GOING TO JERUSALEM.

I HARDLY suppose it possible that any of my readers are ignorant of this old stand-by, but some may have forgotten about it, and so have failed to utilize it.

Arrange a row of chairs alternately facing to the left and the right. Seat the company in them, and let some skilful player preside at the piano. As she begins to play, the company must rise and begin to march around the chairs without halting, keeping step briskly to the music. In the meantime one chair has been removed by a member of the committee, so that, when the music suddenly stops and each scrambles for a seat, one is sure to be left out. Thus the game proceeds until one player is left in solitary glory.

AN OWL SOCIAL.

A SOCIAL of this nature consists of a literary programme largely descriptive of the owl. There is to be a paper describing its habits; recitations connected with the owl like "Jimmy Butler and the Owl," or Sidney Lanier's "Owl Against Robin," and pieces of music such as the college song, "The Owl and the Pussy Cat."

At the close of the literary programme, all members of the company receive pencils and paper. The young men present are condemned to write poems upon owls, and the young women to draw pictures of the same bird. There is to be a committee of men to judge the artistic efforts of the young women, and a committee of women to judge the poetic effusions of the young men. The prizes are to be a paper owl, and a chamois watch-pocket embroidered with owls. The refreshments consist of coffee and "baked owl,"— that is, cookies cut in the shape of an owl.

MRS. BROWN'S TEA.

THIS is an old catch, but may be new to your company. Seat them in a circle, and let the leader announce that Mrs. Brown does not like tea. The player next to him must ask what she *does* like, and the third player must promptly name some article of diet. If this food contains the letter *t*, the leader will cause him ignominiously to leave the circle. Again he will assert that Mrs. Brown does not like tea. Again the question will be raised what she does like, and the next player must name some other article of diet. If it is "bread," that is deemed satisfactory; if "toast," he also is dropped; and so it goes on until all have discovered the secret.

MEAL-BAG RACE.

OBTAIN a number of stout sacks that will reach to the shoulders of the victims. Call for volunteer contestants and place them in these sacks, tying the necks thereof with stout cord about the necks of the players. At the word, "Go," they set off, hopping and tumbling over one another, toward a goal on the other side of the room.

A three-legged race is almost equally comical. Arrange your contestants in pairs, tying the right leg of one to the left leg of the other. Success in this race requires an excellent balance both of body and of temper.

SPOONS.

A TEN or fifteen minutes' interval in the evening's amusement may be filled with this little bit of fun. Blindfold one member of the company, and place him in a chair in the middle of the room. Let one after another of the Endeavorers go up to him, and feed him three teaspoonfuls of water, he endeavoring to guess who is feeding him. When he succeeds, the person he has guessed must take his place.

Another comical performance of a similar nature is the blindfolding of two players, who are seated on the floor opposite each other. One is given a spoon and a peeled banana, and required to cut off bits of the banana and feed the other person with them by means of the spoon, — a feat by no means easy of accomplishment. A saucer full of cracker crumbs may be used instead of the banana. Take pains to cover the carpet with newspapers!

WHO ARE YOU?

ONE player leaves the room, and in his absence is assigned the character of some famous person. On his return he is hailed with questions addressed to him as if he were that person, and from these questions he must guess who he is. In the reverse of this game, entitled, "Who Am I?" the player who withdraws selects his own character, returns, and acts it out until some one has guessed it.

A GUESSING TOURNAMENT.

The various guessing games mentioned in "Social Evenings" and in this volume may be combined to form an elaborate contest. Arrange a series of tables about which the players are to be grouped. At each table one of the guessing contests is to be conducted.

At table No. 1 may be played the penny game described in "Social Evenings" under the head of "Penny Socials." On table No. 2 may be ten bags, each containing objects difficult to distinguish by the touch. The hands must be inserted in these bags, and their contents discerned without the aid of the eye.

Table No. 3 may contain ten Mother Goose pictures. The contestants must ransack the memories of childhood and write for each the appropriate rhyme. Table No. 4 will have a set of baby photographs of ten of the best-known persons present, whose identity must be discovered.

Table No. 5 will contain, written on bits of cardboard, parodies on the names of various well-known young people. Mr. Barker, for example, will appear as "A good watcher, but poor neighbor"; Miss Walker will be "A good pedestrian," and the like. Table No. 6 will have upon it ten pictures of famous people to be recognized.

Table No. 7 will contain drawings representing in some enigmatic way the titles of famous books. Table No. 8 will contain a set of portions of advertisements, arranged according to the instructions given elsewhere in this book. Table No. 9 will test the sense of taste, and table No. 10 the sense of smell.

The players will make the circuit of these tables in order, passing from one to another at the tap of a bell. They will be furnished with cards on which they will record their guesses. When all have been tested in these various ways, correct lists will be read, and each will keep account of the number of correct guesses he has made, will sum them up, and announce them when his name is called. The social committee may honor in some appropriate way the young man and the young woman whose papers are most accurate.

BIBLE PAIRS.

IN "Social Evenings" I have described an interesting and instructive game that I named, "Who Am I?" A pleasant variation, especially useful when it is desired to separate the party into couples for refreshments or other reasons, is the following.

The social committee will write upon pieces of paper the names of Bible men and women that are closely associated together, such as Adam and Eve, Sarah and Abraham, Isaac and Rachel, Jacob and Rebecca, Samson and Delilah, David and Michal, Mary and Joseph, Zacharias and Elizabeth, Martha and Lazarus, Ahab and Jezebel. As the members enter, pin these names upon their backs, giving the young women the female names and the young men the masculine.

By conversation each must discover who he is, and then transfer the paper from his back to the front of his coat. For the final step of the game he must hunt around and discover the name that is mated with his own. The couples thus formed must present themselves for verification to the chairman of the social committee.

INITIALS.

It is easy to obtain sets of cards on which are printed letters of the alphabet. Place these in the hands of some quick-witted person with a versatile brain. Seated in front of the company he will call for the name of some author, artist, soldier, plant, city, gem, — anything, in fact, he pleases, — beginning with — and here he will turn up the letter, and announce it. The first one who fulfils the requirement will receive the letter.

If, for example, quite ignorant of what letter he might turn up, he should say, "Name a capital of one of the United States beginning with —— C," the player who cried out immediately, "Columbus," would receive the card. The one who holds the most cards on the conclusion of the game is victorious.

HUNT THE RING.

Provide a long cord, and, seating the players in a circle, let each grasp the cord with both hands, bringing the hands together and separating them with a rhythmic motion, so that they touch the hands of their neighbors. Somewhere on the cord is strung a gold ring, and this is slyly passed from hand to hand, the constant motion cleverly hiding the transfer. It is the business of a player in the centre to discover where the ring is, and the person with whom the ring is discovered must take his place in the centre. If the company is large, two rings may be used, started at different points on the cord.

Dispensing with the ring and the string, a coin may be used, all the players constantly making the motion of taking a coin from the hand of the neighbor on the right and placing it in the hand of the neighbor on the left.

HYPNOTISM.

It will be easy to turn the thoughts of the company toward hypnotism, and some one may profess to be able to hypnotize any one in the audience. This player should be one who is able to control his countenance and talk fluently. He will induce some one to present himself as a subject.

The subject will be seated in a chair, and after various passes and manifest failure, accompanied by anxious questions as to whether the subject experiences any peculiar sensations, the operator will state that, as he is a difficult subject, it is necessary for him to rise and go to the window, placing his hand upon the glass.

He will then proceed with his passes, and ask, with the greatest solicitude, "Do you feel a pain?" Of course the player will reply that he does not; but the operator must insist that he does, and will keep this up until he finds it best to ask him, "Why, what's that your hand is on?"

UNITED STATES MAIL.

PLACE the chairs at equal distances, and in each a player. These players choose the names of cities of the United States, and the leader, who must have a good memory, will begin the game by calling out, for instance, "Buffalo and San Francisco." These two cities will now change places, and if the leader can possess himself of either vacant seat in the course of the exchange, the person thus ousted must be leader in his turn. When the leader calls "General Delivery," every one must move to some new seat, and the person that is left without a seat is the new leader.

The old game of stage-coach is played in much the same way, except that different parts of the stage-coach and its various passengers, the horses, and so on, are selected by the players, and the leader must improvise a story introducing as many of these names as possible. As the name of each player is introduced, he must rise and whirl around, resuming his seat. When the leader says "Stage-coach," the whole company must go through this performance, and when the climax of a breakdown is reached, all change places, and in the *mêlée* the story-teller finds a chair, thus forcing a new story-teller to the front.

AN ELECTRIC SOCIAL.

EVERY person of intelligence is interested in the growing marvels of electricity, and the subtle fluid has so permeated modern life that in every town is to be found at least one electrician, with some sort

SOCIALS AND GAMES.   121

of electrical apparatus, — telegraph, telephone, electric light, or electric car. The school teachers also can help you out with apparatus and explanations.

Collect everything bearing upon electricity you can find. Especially provide yourselves with strong batteries, and place these in full view of the audience. If you can get different kinds of batteries and some one to explain their difference, so much the better. A machine for the development of frictional electricity, some Leyden jars, Crookes tubes, and the like, will be of great interest. A telegraph instrument with an operator may most easily be procured. Run the lines around the room, and use, if you can, the regular insulators and poles.

Select the wag of your society to manipulate the instrument, — and it makes no difference, for the nonce, whether he understands telegraphy or not. He is to pretend to receive messages which are sent him by some one outside. These messages he will write out upon regular telegraph blanks, deliver them to an attendant, who is dressed as a district messenger boy, and who will hand them to the proper persons. These are expected to read them aloud at once, and, if they are carefully prepared, they will add much to the pleasure of the evening.

This performance may be arranged to enliven the more serious portions of the programme, which will consist of talks upon different phases of electricity and of electrical engineering, and upon the various instruments you may have on exhibition. Of course one of the most exciting moments of the evening will be brought about by a shock, administered to all who can be persuaded to join hands.

A PANSY SOCIAL.

UPON the invitations or announcements may be printed or painted pansies, while the card may read simply:—

FOR THOUGHTS.

In the Christian Endeavor Room of the Westminster Church.

Monday Evening, May 1, eight o'clock.

The first game of the evening may be the catch, "Pansy," described in "Social Evenings." This will break up all stiffness.

Then may come the "Thought" game. A large paper pansy will be hung up where all can see it, and upon it will be written such questions as these: "What can we do to add to the interest of our society? How can we further the work of our church? What is the funniest story you ever heard?" A pencil and card will be handed to each one, and all will be asked to write out their thoughts upon these questions. The contributions will then be exchanged and read.

Quotations about pansies may be written on cards, which will then be cut in two in odd shapes, one half given to a young woman and the other half to a young man. Just before refreshments these may be matched, in order to obtain partners for that interesting occupation.

A SILVER SOCIAL.

THE Iowa Endeavorers that originated this social wrote the invitations on thin paper, which was placed in peanut shells tied prettily with ribbon. The following jingle was written upon the paper: —

> Sir, or madam, as you please,
> In a nutshell me you find,
> Lightly crumpled with a squeeze;
> Very good my word to mind,
> Every one by me invited,
> Read with care; I'll not be slighted.
>
> Silver Social's what I read,
> Oskaloosa, November 4th,
> Come and help supply our need,
> In the chapel of the church.
> A piece of silver kindly bring,
> Light then of heart we'll play and sing.

Of course the main point of the evening will be the gathering of this silver offering, but a very pleasant evening's entertainment may have relation to silver. In the first place, silver paper may be used in the decorations of the room. There may be tables on which will be ranked all kinds of silver curios, — old-fashioned pieces of silver, souvenir spoons, silver ornaments, — everything made of silver that can be brought together, new as well as old. A collection of silver coins of different nationalities would excite much interest.

For the literary part of the programme there may be a debate between the advocates of silver and of gold, or between the monometallists and bimetallists of the society. There may be an open parliament, each member being expected to come prepared to tell one curious thing connected with silver. Some one who is well informed may give a talk about the history of coins. Some one who has travelled in the silver States may tell about the mining industry, and pictures may be exhibited, either engravings or magic lantern views.

THE FARMYARD.

THE leader will give whispered instructions to the different players, telling them what farmyard fowl to represent by making the appropriate noise as loudly as possible when the leader's hand is raised, and by ceasing instantly as soon as the leader's hand is lowered. The person to whom is assigned the character of donkey, however, is not told anything about the silence required when the leader's hand is lowered; and so, when the cackling, crowing, whinnying, quacking, bleating, and mooing are instantly hushed, the donkey's bray sounds with startling distinctness all alone, to the vast amusement of all but the unfortunate victim.

AN IMPERSONATION SOCIAL.

SOME Presbyterian Endeavorers held what they called an "impersonation social," whose nature may be clearly gathered from the following circular, which they sent out beforehand: —

Choose some character you think you can impersonate.

Choose some person of history or of fiction, or some type of mankind.

Be like the person chosen in dress or conversation, or both.

Let your choice be some character familiar to the public.

Use your ingenuity to the utmost to preserve your identity and yet not to mystify others.

The above is merely a guide. Vary the instructions to suit yourself, but please do not go to extremes.

Remember, our object is to have a good time, and the more ready you are to take part, the better time some one else will have.

Don't be afraid that you will know too much concerning the person you have chosen to impersonate. Read up, and be full of facts about yourself as a historical character.

Two prizes will be awarded: one to the most appropriately dressed person, and one to the person guessing the identity of the most people.

Come yourself, and bring others.

Refreshments will be served, and an appropriate entertainment provided.

THEATRICAL ADJECTIVES.

For the ten games that follow I am indebted to an exceedingly bright collection of home amusements, "Fagots for the Fireside," by Lucretia P. Hale, of which Houghton, Mifflin & Co. are the publishers. I have greatly condensed her vivacious accounts, and have changed several of the games, in order to adapt them more completely to the needs of our Christian Endeavor socials.

To play theatrical adjectives, one person must retire from the room while the remainder choose an adjective. Upon his return he must judge what this adjective is by the manner in which the company answer his questions. If the adjective, for example, is "somnolent," the answers will be exceedingly sleepy. If it is "fidgety," there will be no end of jerks and uneasiness under his cross-examination. If it is "startling," not only will the replies be highly imaginative, but they will be given in a decidedly explosive style. The person whose answer gives the clue to the adjective must retire in his turn.

PREPOSTEROUS TRAVEL.

THE company is seated in a circle, and the leader whispers to his right-hand neighbor the name of the country to which he intends travelling. He then asks his left-hand neighbor whether he is to go by land or sea, inquires of the next person what sort of conveyance is to carry him, and of the next towards what point of the compass he is to direct that conveyance.

Then his right-hand neighbor will announce the goal of his intended journey and it will be his duty to explain satisfactorily how he can reach it in the way proposed. For example, if he has secretly declared his intention to go to London, and is told to go by land, on a toboggan, setting out south, he may be compelled to go by way of the South Pole, and to establish some very eccentric bridges, on sloping trestle-work. It will be seen that this game affords abundant scope for the imagination.

LITERATI.

ONE player having withdrawn, the others decide on the name of some prominent person, — for example, "Lincoln." L is assigned to one player, *i* to the next, *n* to the third, and so on. When the player is called from the other room, he questions the one who has the first letter, and who must answer his questions having in mind the name of some person whose name begins with *l*, such as Lowell. The questioner must try to find out what person he is thinking of. If this is accomplished, he knows that the company has thought of some name beginning with *l*.

Passing to the next player, who may choose for his character Isaac, he will endeavor to discover in the same way the second letter of the name thought of by the company. N may be Newton; *c*, Cæsar; *o*, Obadiah; *l*, Lucy Larcom; and *n*, Nebuchadnezzar. If this series of questions fails to disclose the name desired, the leader may go on around the circle, new characters being taken whose names begin with the letters in the word Lincoln. The person who has given the final hint leading to the discovery of this name must withdraw next.

QUOTATIONS.

SEAT the company in opposite rows, the leader of one of which must begin the game by quoting a line or more from some poet. Before he is through with the quotation some one on the opposite side must name the author from whom he is quoting. In default of this the leader has the privilege of choosing some player from the opposite side. It is now the turn of the head of the opposing column to give a quotation, and so the game proceeds down the rows, the quotations alternating from side to side.

The same game may be played in reverse order by permitting each player to select a poet from whom he will be ready to give quotations when called upon. The company is seated in a circle, and, standing in the centre with a plate, the leader twirls it, at the same time calling the name of one of the poets chosen, whose representative must give a quotation before the plate falls. Failing to do this, he must take his place in the centre, and spin the plate until he also catches some one napping.

ALPHABET STORIES.

SET the entire company to composing stories of twenty-six words, the first letters of the words being, in order, the letters of the alphabet. One of Miss Hale's samples is the following: " A Barbarous Caterpillar Destroyed Every Fuchsia Growing Here In June, Killing Likewise Many New Orchids Planted Quite Recently. Such Totally Unexpected Villainous Work Xasperated Young Zebedee."

The alphabet also could be used backward, after this fashion: "Zealous Young Xantippe, Wedded Very Unhappily To Socrates, Reiterated Querulous Personalities On Noted Men Like Kleon, Jealously Insulting Husband, Greece, Friends, Every Dear Creature, By Abusive, Angry Aspersions."

I LOVE MY LOVE.

The old form of this game is played in this way. The leader begins with, "I love my love with an A because he (or *she*, according to the sex of the speaker) is Amiable. I hate him, because he is Audacious. He took me to the sign of the Antelope, and gave me Apples to eat and Ale to drink. His name is Anthony, and he came from Albany." The next player must go through the same formula using the letter B, and so on through the alphabet.

Miss Hale's variation is ingenious. It requires the use of the initials, either two, or all three, of any person present. Here is her example: "I love my love with an A. S. F. because she has A Sweet Face. I hate her (if possible) because she is an Anti-Suffrage Female. I took her to the sign of the Anglo-Saxon Farmer, and gave her A Spring Fowl to eat and All-Spice Flip to drink. She reads the Anti-Socialist Federalist, and smells of A Sweet Flower. Her name is Annie Sturtevant Fortescue, and she comes from Augustine (St.), Florida."

THE TRAVELLING BEAN BAGS.

Permit two leaders to choose up, each calling to his side one-half the company. All the members of one side will pin upon themselves white badges, and the other side will be designated with red. Lines are now to be formed, one headed by the white captain, the other by the red, while the various colors will alternate down the line.

Each captain will be provided with a cloth bag of beans containing about half a pint. At a given signal the white captain throws his bag to the white man opposite, and he diagonally to the second white man in the opposite row, and so on, the bean bag zigzagging down the rows to the end, and then back to the leader. The side that succeeds first in accomplishing this task is victorious.

The game may be made more difficult by using ten bags on a side, and sending them down the line one after the other. To avoid confusion, the bags of one side should be of white cloth and those of the other side of red.

APPRENTICE MY SON.

THE leader begins by saying, "I apprenticed my son to a stationer, and the first thing he sold was a C. P. C." The company must guess what article the young apprentice disposed of, and the fortunate guesser of a *celluloid paper-cutter* has the privilege in his turn of apprenticing a son.

SONNETS.

ANY sonnet from any poet is to be selected, the name of the poet and title of the sonnet being kept a secret. One at a time the final word of each line is to be disclosed to the company. As each concluding word is announced, the players are required to write a line of ten syllables ending with that word, and all must accomplish the task before the word that terminates the next line is disclosed.

The game will be made more difficult, though the result will not be so varied, if a topic for all sonnets is assigned beforehand. Probably it will be best to permit each player to choose his own theme.

CAT'S CONCERT.

For a five-minute relief from more serious games, gather the entire company in a group, and permit them, on a signal from the leader, to sing at the top of their voices, each one a different tune.

ALLITERATION.

Mr. V. G. Mays is the author of the following pleasant adaptation of the common game of alliteration. He suggests that upon cards should be placed the letters of the alphabet. If more than twenty-six are present at the social, these letters may be repeated. The more difficult letters, like x, y, z, j, and q, may be omitted. The players choose their cards by lot, and on a given signal are set to writing sentences, each word of which must begin with the letter upon the card. If the committee choose to grant this privilege, the players may be allowed to incorporate in the sentences one or two connectives beginning with some other letter. On the expiration of the allotted time, the sentences are read, and the person who has written the longest is adjudged victor.

A variation of this entertainment requires the social committee to form beforehand a number of alliterative sentences, each based upon a different letter. The sentences are cut apart, and the words composing them given to the different members of the company, who are required to get together in groups, each group bearing words beginning with the same letter. These words are to be compared, and put together by the group in the proper order, the group first succeeding being accounted victors.

The first game may be varied by dividing the company into groups, the members of each group competing with one another as to who shall form the longest sentence. Or the entire company may be divided into two sets, and the same letter assigned to each set. The side that produces within a given time the longest sentence beginning with that letter has the privilege of choosing one from the opposite side. A new letter is assigned, and so the game proceeds until one side is reduced to naught.

Another pleasant variation is the writing of alliterative stories consisting of as many sentences as the writer pleases. In this case it is best to assign a topic for all the stories, such as Columbus setting the egg on end, Newton and the apple, Franklin and the kite, or the fable of the fox and the grapes.

AN UMBRELLA SOCIAL.

PRESENT all that come with tiny Japanese parasols upon which are written questions relating to missions, preferably to Japanese missions, especially if your denomination has missions in that country. Half of the parasols contain the questions, and half the answers to the same questions. Have a bright programme consisting of papers and talks and possibly songs relating to the country you have chosen. On the conclusion of this, let each that has a question read it, and those that hold the answers, or think they hold them, read them. Much missionary information can be gained in this way.

A PHOTOGRAPH SOCIAL.

LET every one that comes to the social be requested to bring a photograph of himself, — one taken so long ago, or at a time when he was so different in appearance, that the photograph will not be likely to be recognized. As he enters he will give the photograph to an attendant, passing on to deposit hat or wraps. Returning to the room where the social is held, on entering each selects at random another photograph, whose owner he must discover in the course of the evening, seeking also to identify as many other photographs as possible. For additional amusement on this evening the social committee might make use of the photograph social described in "Social Evenings."

A FACULTY SOCIAL.

THIS amusement under various names is quite well known, and if your society has not tried it, you will find it an excellent plan for passing a pleasant hour. Each of the five senses is to be tested in turn. To test the sight, cover a table with a miscellaneous collection of objects as incongruous as possible. The Endeavorers are filed slowly past this table, being bidden to look at everything, if possible, and to carry them all away in memory. Each is furnished with paper and pencil, and makes out a list of all objects on the table, so far as his memory will serve him.

Another form of this test we may give the eye is the following. Fill ten little dishes with various substances, such as sugar, powdered cinnamon, ground sulphur, white pepper, ground coffee, sand, borax, and the like, requiring the Endeavorers to tell by looking at these substances what they are.

To test the hearing, ten different musical instruments are sounded in a neighboring room. If thought best they may be sounded together, and from the tangle the Endeavorers be required to distinguish each of the ten instruments. The word "instrument" is used in a loose sense, since it may include tin pans, cow-bells, sleigh-bells, and the like!

Next, ten little bottles filled with substances of various odors are passed about the room, the stronger odors, like camphor and ammonia, being slyly passed first. Each is required to make a list of these as they reach him.

The tongue is to be tested by the passing of various packages, each of which is to be tasted. The substance should be disguised to the eye; for example, popcorn may be pounded so as to appear a powder. Water may be carefully dropped from a colored bottle, and will deceive not a few. Substances commonly found in powders may be stuck together in cakes.

To test the touch, darken the room and pass from one to another ten different objects, such as a cold buckwheat pancake, a pig's tail, a kid glove stuffed with wet sand, a piece of resin, a bit of tortoise-shell, and the like. After the light is restored, the players are required to make a list of these objects, so far as they have guessed them. Another form of the latter test is to place ten different objects under a cloth, and require the players to feel around until they have discovered ten objects. This is not so funny, however, as the first plan.

After these five tests a correct list is read. Each player checks his neighbor's list, and then it is announced how many each has guessed correctly. Some appropriate reward should be given to the best guesser for each test.

LIVING AUTHORS.

FOUR players are to be given the names of poets, four of novelists, four of essayists, four of historians, four of humorists, and so on. Each player is told in secret whom he is to represent. The complete list is placed before the society, plainly printed upon a blackboard.

These preliminaries being arranged, from four to seven or eight unnamed persons play the game. They sit in a circle, and draw their cards by calling in turn upon the members to stand behind their chair. As each member reaches the chair he whispers to the player his author's name.

The game proceeds as in the well-known game of authors, each player calling in turn for an author needed to complete some book of which he has a part. After a book is formed, it is made to sit down behind the chair of the fortunate player, and so the game proceeds until all are seated.

EGG FOOT-BALL.

To play this amusing game, carefully blow out the contents of a hen's egg. Group your players around a piano or a large table, place the egg in the centre, and station at either end two uprights for the goal posts. Four salt cellars will answer the purpose.

Divide the company into two "teams," that may be called respectively the Yales and the Harvards, and let the members of these bands alternate. On a given signal all are to blow upon the egg with all their might, each band striving to blow the egg through the goal posts of their opponents. The team first succeeding in this is victorious.

For a social several groups might be set to playing this game simultaneously, or you might ask all present to form themselves into teams representing their favorite colleges, and carry on a series of games on a single field, for the championship.

A BIBLE TEST.

Here is a well-known alphabet of Scripture proper names which may be utilized at a social by ranking

SOCIALS AND GAMES. 137

the members on two sides, and reading these lines one at a time, in the same way that a spelling bee is carried on: —

A was a monarch who reigned in the East;
(Esth. 1: 1.)
B was a Chaldee who made a great feast;
(Dan. 5: 1-4.)
C was veracious, when others told lies;
(Num. 13: 30-33.)
D was a woman heroic and wise;
(Judg. 4: 4-14.)
E was a refuge, where David spared Saul;
(1 Sam. 24: 1-7.)
F was a Roman, accuser of Paul;
(Acts 26: 24.)
G was a garden, a favorite resort;
(John 18: 1-2; Matt. 26: 36.)
H was a city where David held court;
(2 Sam. 2: 11.)
I was a mocker, a very bad boy;
(Gen. 16: 16.)
J was a city, preferred as a joy;
(Ps. 137: 6.)
K was a father, whose son was quite tall;
(1 Sam. 9: 1, 2.)
L was a proud one, who had a great fall;
(Isa. 14: 12.)
M was a nephew, whose uncle was good;
(Col. 4: 10; Acts 11: 24.)
N was a city, long hid where it stood;
(Zeph. 2: 13.)
O was a servant, acknowledged a brother;
(Philemon 1-16.)
P was a Christian, greeting another;
(2 Tim. 1: 1, 2.)
R was a damsel, who knew a man's voice;
(Acts 12: 13, 14.)

S was a sovereign who made a bad choice ;
(1 Kings 11 : 4-11.)
T was a seaport, where preaching was long ;
(Acts 20 : 6, 7.)
U was a teamster, struck dead for his wrong ;
(2 Sam. 6: 7.)
V was a cast-off, and never restored ;
(Esth. 1: 19.)
Z was a ruin, with sorrow deplored ;
(Ps. 137: 1.)

For several of the descriptions more than one person will answer, and if a good reply is made it should be accepted, whether it is the one expected or not.

A BIBLE SOCIAL.

ANY biblical theme may be made the basis of a social. Take, for instance, faith. Papers may be read on Bible heroes of faith. There may be a talk on faith by the pastor, appropriate music may be sung, and poems recited.

The parables of Christ would furnish material for an evening's thought and profitable entertainment. There are many poems based upon these parables that could be repeated, and many helpful papers could be written upon themes suggested by the immortal stories. Pictures illustrating them could be grouped on the walls. You could have a question match based on the parables. Each Endeavorer might be required to come representing in some way one of the parables, — having a piece of money strung around his neck, carrying a handful of seed, eating husks, or the like.

This is a mere hint of a vast range of delightful socials that any wide-awake committee might contrive.

NOTED MEN.

Give to each paper and pencils, and require him to write a list, as long as he can make it in two minutes, of noted men whose last names begin with A. On the expiration of the time, each reads his list, and scores one for every player in the room that has not a name that he himself has. If, for example, his list contains Alfred Austin, and six persons in the room have failed to record the poet laureate, that name will count him six. The count being completed, the company goes to B, and so on.

ANIMAL CONSEQUENCES.

Each player draws upon a piece of paper the head of some animal, and folds it so as to leave in sight only the lower portion of the neck. Upon this his neighbor, to whom the paper is passed, fits the body of any animal he may think of, and folds it so as to leave in sight only a line or two indicating where the legs are to be joined on. Once more the papers are passed, and the pictures are concluded by the addition of legs. The results will, of course, be fantastic enough, as an elephant's head, gifted with a swan's body and a dog's feet.

A MODELLING PARTY.

Give to each guest a square of cardboard, to which is fastened, by a string through one end, a sharpened pencil, and to the other end a generous piece of chewing gum. While the company are in the midst of conjectures as to what this combination means, request each to write in the middle of his piece of cardboard the name of some animal. This being accomplished, inform the company that each is to mould the gum in the shape of the animal he has named. Modelling clay may be used in place of the gum, but is not quite so easily managed.

This operation will produce much merriment. Many of the animals will be very lifelike, and many others quite the reverse. When all have completed their artistic tasks, they are to place the products of their skill upon a table in the centre of the room.

Below each animal must be the cardboard belonging to it, with the name of the animal downward. Upon the upper surface the social committee will write a number, and cards, upon which is a corresponding list of numbers, will be given each player. Opposite each number the players are to write the name of the animal they think the sculptor intended to represent. The social committee will correct these lists, or read a correct list and have the members correct their own guesses. The most accurate list may be rewarded with a toy animal.

MAGIC MUSIC

A PLAYER must withdraw, and in his absence the company fix upon some part of the room to which he must go, and something he must do when he gets there. Seating herself at the piano, one player directs his motions when he enters by playing softly when he goes in the wrong direction or does the wrong thing, and loudly when he gets "hot." It is astonishing how speedily a quick-witted player can in this way guess the design of the others.

NOVELS.

A WRITER in *The Congregationalist* describes this game. The players are furnished with sheets of paper, at the top of which each writes the name of an imaginary novel. Turning it down so that the next player cannot see what has been written, he passes the sheet on. All are then required to complete the titles with subtitles, in a similar manner passing the sheet on after the insertion of this important feature. The next item is the name of the hero, then a heroine is furnished, and then the novel is summed up in a sentence or two containing a climax, and finally a brief criticism on the whole is written, after which the papers are given to one player to read aloud, or else are read aloud in turn by those who happen to hold them.

Here is a sample of the result: —

The Story of a Fat Tramp,
Or,
A Doughnut's Revenge.
Hero: Father.
Heroine: My kitty.

What happened? The Indian shot the white man with seven deadly arrows.

Criticism: The book will be enjoyed by young and old

alike, of both sexes and of all nationalities. It is replete with wit and harrowing detail. To be had at any news-stand for ten cents.

A COOKY SOCIAL.

The keynote of the social will be given as the members arrive, by a large pumpkin lantern placed over the door. Instead of the customary grinning face, the C. E. monogram will gleam out.

Get one of the boys to make a cooky-cutter shaped like the same monogram. With the aid of this, prepare a large number of C. E. monogram cookies.

The game that will open the social and give to it its name will thus be carried out. Place upon one wall of the room, at some distance from the spectators, a number of paper C. E. monograms and one cooky monogram, all made to look as much alike as possible. Number these, and call upon the members present to guess which monogram is a cooky. On the conclusion of the guesses give the members an invitation to come forward, take the monogram they have fixed upon, and eat it!

A PORTRAIT SOCIAL.

From the portrait catalogues of book publishers and the illustrated weeklies, as well as from the magazines, may be obtained a large number of portraits of famous men and women. Cut these out neatly, and paste them carefully upon uniform squares of cardboard. Number these, and perforate them at the top for bits of ribbon by which they may be fastened to the coats and dresses of the players. Each player is also furnished with a piece of cardboard bearing a list of numbers, as many as there are portraits in the room.

The players are expected to fill their cards with a correct list of the persons represented by the various portraits, each name opposite the proper number. If the company is large, this operation will require at least an hour. On the close of it the cards are handed to a committee, who will examine them. In the meantime some pleasant literary or musical exercise may be given, closed by the announcement of the committee.

DATES.

LET the social committee prepare a list of dates on which well-known events occurred and read these dates slowly, giving the company time to write on slips of paper the events they think occurred on those dates. This being accomplished, a correct list will be read, the members revising their own and reporting the number they have right. A pretty box of dates would be an appropriate prize for the victor, and for the booby prize an old, dog's-eared school history.

JACK HORNER AND HIS PIE.

AN amusing and at the same time profitable feature of a social may be contrived by means of a large imitation pie. Get a pan, the most generous you can find, divide it into compartments, and fill these compartments with various articles that are to be sold. The most roomy division may be filled with candy. Pen-wipers, pin-cushions, needle-books, thimbles, paper weights, paper cutters, and the like, may fill the other compartments.

Attach to each object a string, which is allowed to hang down outside. Above the whole place a cover of brown paper, made to imitate pie crust, and cut in sections that can be lifted separately. Dress some comical little boy to look like the traditional Jack Horner, and set him in the corner with the pie before him. Charge a small fee for the privilege of selecting a string, which Jack Horner is to pull, extracting the plum, which the brave boy will hand over to the purchaser for his own delectation. Of course with each pull Jack will give vent to the traditional exclamation.

UP JENKINS.

This is an old-fashioned game, suitable for a small party, or for a subdivision of a large social. Set the players close together around a large table, the halves facing one another to be contestants. To one side is given a silver half-dollar. They pass it from hand to hand very quickly under the table until Number One on the opposite side calls out, "Up Jenkins."

Immediately every hand on the side with the coin must be raised, and laid squarely upon the table. Care must be taken, of course, by the one who happens to hold the coin, not to betray that fact by ringing it on the table as his hand goes down, or by fumbling it in the process.

Number One on the opposite side, if his sharp eye has discovered the location of the coin, or if he has a good guess at it, will proceed to call up the hands before him, saying, " Up John's right hand, up Jennie's left hand," and so on, aiming to leave on the table for the last the hand under which is the coin. In that case his own side take their turn at the sport. If he fails, the first side goes through the same process again, and Number Two of their opponents tries his hand at the discovery. The side that scores the fewest failures, beats.

A POPCORN SOCIAL.

This is a social for the Juniors, who will be interested in helping to prepare the material beforehand. Decorate the room with strings of popcorn, and also with ears of corn not popped. Popcorn may be sold in various forms, — balls, bricks, plain, sugared, and so on. The older Endeavorers may be invited to make this part of the social a success. The popcorn-eating contest mentioned in " Social Evenings " will make a brisk addition to this social.

AN ANIMAL SOCIAL.

This will please the Juniors. Assign to different members of the society recitations upon animals to be given, or compositions upon different animals to be written and read. For a competition, pass around among the Juniors present folded sheets of paper. On one half of the sheet is to be drawn an animal, and on the other half must be written a description of the same animal.

After all are through, let description and drawing be handed in to the superintendent, who will tear them apart. Pin the drawings upon the wall, distribute the descriptions among the Juniors haphazard, and set each to seeking the picture belonging to the description. A little prize of some toy animal might be given to the author and artist that does the best. Little animal crackers might form part of the refreshments.

A UNION CONVERSAZIONE.

This social is especially useful where you have a gathering of several societies. Divide them into groups of six or eight each, seated around a table. Assign to each group a leader, who will maintain his position at the table throughout the evening, directing the conversation there.

Each table is to discuss some live Christian Endeavor topic, such as the best way of raising money for missions, the most important elements in a good prayer meeting, the faults of society singing and how to remedy them, the pledge and how to keep it. At the end of the first five minutes, half of each group must be sent to another table, and so the company is to be kept in circulation until each member has met all the others.

At each table is to be seated a reporter, who will remain there throughout the evening, taking notes of the helpful points brought out in the conversation at that table. After all the Endeavorers have made the circuit of the tables, these reporters will give their

SOCIALS AND GAMES. 147

reports. The others should have a chance to add to these summings-up, if anything interesting or helpful has been omitted.

A VALENTINE SUPPER.

One Christian Endeavor society used the following menu at a Valentine supper, the participants ordering from these enigmatic hints.

....MENU....

My Stay Through Life.
I Fly To Thee, 5 cents.   Forever Thine, 5 cents.
Beat That Ball, 5 cents.
Love Antidote, and True Lover's Knot, 5 cents.

DESSERT.

Midsummer's Dream, 10 cents.
My Mother Loves Thee and My Father Does Not Object, 5 cents.
Odd Commodities.

DRINKS.

African Beauty, 5 cents.   Chinese Heartease, 5 cents.
Squeeze Me More, 5 cents.
Elixir of Life.

With the exception of the "Odd Commodities," which was a mixture of fruits, the interpretation of the menu in order was the following: " Bread, chicken, cold beef, beets and potato balls, pickles, crullers, ice cream, apple pie and pumpkin pie, coffee, tea, lemonade, water."

A FAGOT PARTY.

GIVE to each Endeavorer that will accept it under the conditions, a bundle of sticks tied in a fagot. The conditions are that the fagot must be placed in an open fire-place, — and the room must contain one, if this form of social is to be used, — and while the fagot is burning the member that deposited it must tell a story, the story to be at least as long as the life of the fagot.

AN INDOOR PICNIC.

TRY the plan of holding an Endeavor picnic during the winter months. Decorate the room in which you meet with as much green as possible, and spread the viands upon the floor, or, if you choose, on tables. Have everything brought in covered baskets, one basket to a table — or to a tablecloth. You may cut up quotations into four or eight parts, requiring the holders of these parts to eat together.

NEEDLES AND THREAD.

FOR a few minutes' sport during a social, provide needles and thread, and announce the contest, requesting the young men to volunteer. Those that have sufficient daring are provided each with ten needles and a long thread, upon which, at the word, "Go," they must proceed to string the needles, making a knot after each needle. The one who first accomplishes the task is adjudged the victor, and is to be adorned with a large bow of bright red ribbon.

A UNION SOCIAL.

A GOOD plan for a union social was once described by a writer in *The Advance*. As the various persons enter they give their names to a set of quick writers, who prepare for each a card on which his name is written as an anagram, — "Martine," for instance, being transformed into "raiment"; or in which the name is described in some punning fashion, Mr. Paine, for example, being represented by a face with agonized expression, and swollen, bandaged jaws; or by a rebus in which, for instance, Mr. R. A. Underwood's name is written

Wood
R. A.

As soon as the majority have arrived, these cards are distributed at random, except that care is taken to give cards bearing ladies' names to the gentlemen. Each card-holder is then required to hunt through the company and discover the person whose name is upon his card. This being accomplished, the two must go together in search of the person undiscovered by one of them.

Thus three, at least, are made to know one another, and in the process they must have talked with many more. If thought desirable, there may be at this point a general exchange of cards, resulting in a fresh set of acquaintances.

A RAILROAD SOCIAL.

The society that devised this social sent out invitations reading somewhat like this: "The Y. P. S. C. E. of the Holland Church will give a railroad social on Friday evening. Train will leave the home of Miss Green at eight o'clock. Come in travelling costume. Round trip, ten cents. Train will stop for lunch."

The walls of the rooms that were to represent the cars were decorated with railroad maps and with announcements, such as "Don't flirt with the brakeman"; "Bachelors must not make fun of the bride and groom"; "Every one is permitted to ride on the platform," and the like. The chairs were arranged in rows, with aisles between, in imitation of a car.

At the entrance each traveller paid his ten cents, and received a pasteboard ticket bearing the name of some station. Only two, a young man and a young woman, received tickets to the same station, and they were expected to sit together in the cars. One Endeavorer represented a colored porter, even to the point of demanding a fee for everything he did. There was a train boy, with his packages of candy, his basket of fruit and sandwiches, his paper novels, and his latest magazines. There were brakemen, who called the stations, and a conductor to punch the tickets. There were a few amusing characters, such as the bride and groom, the old farmer taking his first trip upon the train, the Western cow-boy, the fussy old maid with her bundles and birdcage, the crying baby, the fidgety small boy, and so on.

A stop was made for ten minutes at a junction, where was a lunch-counter over which sandwiches and coffee were served, as well as a dining-room where could be obtained in more leisurely fashion ice-cream, cake, and fruit. The hilarity of such a social might well be tempered with several talks on railroading in its various phases, delivered while the train is in motion between the stations. All sorts of accessories, such as engine bells, whistles, signal-flags, and the like, may be introduced.

A PEANUT RACE.

THIS is similar to the well-known potato race, but is more difficult. A pile of peanuts is placed at one end of the room, and at the other, upon chairs, as many dishes as there are contestants. Each is given a large knife, upon which, at a given signal, he scoops up as many peanuts as he can and carries them to his dish at the other end of the room. The one who within the allotted time places the largest number of peanuts in his dish is accounted the victor.

AUCTION.

SELECT your wittiest member for the auctioneer. He will choose a number of the Endeavorers and set them up at auction as if they were statues, giving the statues appropriate names. For example, he will dub a very tall young man " Tom Thumb "; a particularly fragile youth " Corbett or Sullivan "; a pretty young girl "Liliuokalani," and so on. The members of the audience will make their bids, offering all sorts of queer things, such as a toothpick, an old shoe, a comb, a cuff button, a hairpin, or a pocket knife. The bid that succeeds in making the statue laugh is the one that is victorious

A MAGAZINE MEET.

THIS pleasant evening's entertainment was originated by Miss Olive E. Dana. She suggests that each Endeavorer be assigned beforehand some magazine or paper to represent. This is to guard against duplications. All the prominent periodicals are easily represented, with a little ingenuity. For example, a bundle of examination papers which the bearer is assiduously correcting, will stand for *The Review of Reviews;* a tomahawk, with a feather in the hair, would sufficiently indicate *The North American;* a pair of strolling musicians would be *Harper's;* a diary of domestic events, *The Ladies' Home Journal;* a marine view carried in the hand would suggest *The Atlantic; St. Nicholas* would require a long beard, a fur overcoat, and a pack on the back; *The Bazar* might be organized in one corner; a foot rule brightly gilded would stand for the Endeavorers' favorite organ.

After all have admired these various shrewd contrivances, the company may proceed to the more solid portion of the evening, consisting of papers and discussions concerning that important feature of modern life, the magazine. These could be as varied as the ability and interests of the members. One might describe the magazine of our grandfathers' days and bring some old numbers to show. One could tell about the way magazines are illustrated, and the growth of this important feature. There might be a debate in which the claims of the various favorite magazines are presented. Magazine advertisements, famous magazine serials, articles, and series of articles, the lessened price of magazines, the influence of magazines on modern life, — these are samples of topics that might be used.

AN AMATEUR PHOTOGRAPHY SOCIAL.

If your society and church contains a number of enthusiastic amateur photographers, you may successfully make amateur photography the basis of a social.

Appoint these enthusiasts a committee to collect from their friends all their best specimens of work. They may bring in also any remarkable photographs they themselves may happen to have. There will be transparencies, blue prints, out-of-focus photographs, colored photographs, and, in fine, an assortment as varied and attractive as possible. Make a collection also of different kinds of cameras, from the pocket Kodak up.

Photographs should be ranged along the wall in groups, each headed by the name of the exhibitor. There should be a section devoted to old-fashioned portraits, the daguerreotypes and ambrotypes of our grandfathers. At a certain point in the evening, after all have examined these, a vote should be taken as to which shows the best workmanship, and the successful exhibitor should be rewarded with a grotesque wooden medal, presented with a comical speech.

At least half an hour of the evening should be devoted to a careful explanation of the principles of photography, made by some competent person, and illustrated with the apparatus, and with the actual performance, so far as possible, of the processes involved. An opportunity should be given for questions from the audience relative to the cost of cameras, the difficulty of developing the plates, finishing the pictures, and so on.

An open parliament, in which all photographers present will give whatever entertaining experiences they have had in connection with their favorite pursuit, would add to the evening's enjoyment.

AN ADVERTISEMENT SOCIAL.

This is an age of advertisements, and no one can fail to become familiar with the various devices and catch words used by the most vigorous of American manufacturers and retailers. This common knowledge may be very pleasantly utilized in an evening's entertainment.

The social committee will make a collection of all sorts of advertisements, choosing those that are most prominently before the public, such as baking powders, bicycles, typewriters, soaps, patent medicines, shoes, and soups. These are to be cut out and mounted upon sheets of cardboard, no more than five or six on one sheet. Pains must be taken not to include in the portion of the advertisement selected the name of the article, or anything that would give too definite a clue to the name. Well-known phrases, such as " See that hump? " " Good morning; have you used —," " $\frac{99}{100}$ pure," " Absolutely pure," " A little higher in price, but —," " It floats," " That tired feeling," and so on, should by all means be included.

So many of the advertisers use artistic illustrations that your cards will be quite pretty when they are done, especially if some taste is used in grouping the selections. Finally, number the advertisements consecutively, and prepare pieces of cardboard containing lists of numbers up as far as the advertisements go. Place the sheets of advertisements all around the room.

The players will be furnished with paper and pencils, and required to make lists of the articles advertised. Of course they may begin with any sheet. Give them an abundance of time for filling out their cards. The most accurate list may be rewarded with the prettiest advertising calendar you can find, and the poorest with some grotesque advertising bill.

THE END.

INDEX.

	PAGE
Acknowledgment, A Word of	22
Advertisement Social	154
Alliteration	131
Alphabet Stories	128
Amateur Photography Social	153
Animal Consequences	139
Animal Social	145
Animated Portraits	29
Apprentice My Son	130
Art Gallery	61
Auction	151
Authors' Exchange	49
Averages	25
Baby Social	72
Bible Pairs	117
Bible Social	138
Bible Test	136
Birthday Socials	101
Blind Menu	41
Burlesque Banquet	42
Cat's Concert	131
Chalk Talk	30
City Chains	37
Class Receptions	81
Clothes-Pins	45

	PAGE
Commerce	66
Committees Take Turns	59
Conversation Social, Novel,	73
Cooky Social	142
Corn Socials	29
Counting the Words	28
Court, A Queer	79
Dates	143
"D. B. F."	44
Doublets	108
Drawing Contest	54
Egg Foot-Ball	136
Egg Social	39
Electric Social	120
Endeavor Oratory	55
Evening in Greenland	80
Examination, A Queer	94
Faculty Social	133
Fagot Party	148
Farmyard	124
Fern Socials	28
Floral Love Tale	50
Fortune-Telling	36
German Socials	86
Going to Jerusalem	113
Guessing Tournament	116

INDEX.

	PAGE
Halloween Social Programme	35
Hanging	23
Harlequin	99
Harvest Social	75
Heart Party	65
Hit-or-Miss Social	82
Holmes Social	52
Home Mission Social	97
Hunt the Ring	118
Husking-Bee	44
Hypnotism	119
I Love My Love	129
Impersonation Social	124
Indoor Picnic	148
Initials	118
International Tea	105
Introductions	85
Introduction Social	69
It Rests	86
Jack Horner and His Pie	143
Japanese Social	109
Journey by Map	104
Key to Character	98
Lemon Socials	100
Literati	127
Living Authors	135
Magazine Meet	152
Magic Music	140
Meal-Bag Race	114
Memory Game	38
Mind-Reading	89
Missionary Book Social	74
Missionary Games	85
Modelling Party	139
Move, A	50
Mrs. Brown's Tea	114
Needles and Thread	148
New Members' Social	40
Noted Men	139
Nouns and Adjectives	22
Novels	141
Number Groups	58
Nut Social	80
Nutshell, Everything from a,	104
Old Maids' Repair-Shop	98
Old-Time Social	45
Orange Socials	82
Owl Social	113
Pansy Social	122
Paper, The Hidden	36
Patience	33
Peanut Race	151
Photograph Social	133
Picnics, Christian Endeavor,	41
Pie Social	56
Pigeon	31
Poetical Descriptions	92
Political Social	57
Polyglot Social	48
Popcorn Social	145
Portrait Social	142
Post	40
Post-Office Social	56
Poverty Socials, Invitations to	26
Preposterous Travel	126
Progressive Games	88
Quaker	107
Quartette Social	45

INDEX. 159

	PAGE
Questions and Answers	75
Quilting Party	96
Quotations	128
Quotation Social	74
Railroad Social	150
Rainbow Fête	77
Reciprocal	78
Refreshments, Easily Prepared	38
Runaway Feather	37
St. Patrick's Day Social	42
Scripture Autograph Social	88
Ship Social Tickets	90
Significant Initials	25
Silver Social	123
Social Groups	77
Social — to Save	15
Social to Serve	54
Something from All	48
Songs in Pictures	78
Sonnets	130
Spelling-Matches, Old-Fashioned	67
Spoons	115
Stamp Social	52
Statistical Social	70

	PAGE
Steamboat's Coming!	87
Strangers' Socials	74
Tennis Social	72
Theatrical Adjectives	125
Throwing the Handkerchief	97
Toasts	32
To Fit	31
Travelling Bean Bags	129
Trip on the No-Name Line	53
Trolley Parties	24
Umbrella Social	132
Union Conversazione	146
Union Social	149
United States Mail	120
Up Jenkins	144
Valentine Supper	147
Vegetable Social	59
Violet Social	26
War and Peace Social	43
Week in a Day	108
Weight, Their	91
Weights and Ages	68
Where Were You Born?	46
Who Are You?	115
Wishbone Social	102
Wooden Social	47

How To Play.

By Amos R. Wells.

7 1-4 by 4 1-2 inches in size. Bound in cloth, with illuminated cover design. 162 pages. Price, 75 cents.

The author of this book evidently believes in recreation. The very first chapter is entitled, "The Duty of Playing." Separate chapters are devoted to the principal indoor amusements, conversation and reading being the author's preferences, and also to the leading outdoor sports, especially the bicycle and lawn tennis. There are many practical chapters on such themes as how to keep games fresh, inventing games, what true recreation is, and how to use it to the best advantage. "Flabby Playing," "Playing by Proxy," "Fun that Fits," "Overdoing It," —these are some of the chapter titles. In one section of the book scores of indoor games are described, concisely, but with sufficient fulness.

United Society of Christian Endeavor,
Boston and Chicago.

Our Workers' Library

*Cloth bindings, 35 cents each, postpaid.
All twelve volumes, $3.25, postpaid*

These books should be in every Christian Endeavor library. Are they in yours?

THE OFFICERS' HANDBOOK. By Amos R. Wells. A manual for the officers of young people's societies, together with chapters upon parliamentary law, business meetings, etc.

FIFTY MISSIONARY PROGRAMMES. By Belle M. Brain. Valuable suggestions upon ideal missionary meetings, together with fifty entirely different programmes for missionary meetings.

THE MISSIONARY MANUAL. By Amos R. Wells. The most complete handbook of methods for missionary work in young people's societies ever published.

FUEL FOR MISSIONARY FIRES. By Belle M. Brain. Practical plans for missionary committees. Everything tried and proved.

PRAYER-MEETING METHODS. By Amos R. Wells. This book contains by far the most comprehensive collection of prayer-meeting plans ever made.

SOCIAL EVENINGS. By Amos R. Wells. This is the most widely used collection of games and social entertainments ever made.

SOCIAL TO SAVE. By Amos R. Wells. A companion volume to "Social Evenings." A mine of enjoyment for the society and home circle.

OUR UNIONS. By Amos R. Wells. Wholly devoted to Christian Endeavor unions of all kinds, their officers, work, and conventions.

WEAPONS FOR TEMPERANCE WARFARE. By Belle M. Brain. Full of ammunition for temperance meetings. Hundreds of facts, illustrations, suggestions, programmes.

NEXT STEPS. By Rev. W. F. McCauley. A book for every Christian Endeavor worker. It is a storehouse of suggestions.

CITIZENS IN TRAINING. By Amos R. Wells. A complete manual of Christian citizenship.

EIGHTY PLEASANT EVENINGS. A book of social entertainments intended for young people's societies, church workers, temperance unions, and for individual use.

United Society of Christian Endeavor,

Tremont Temple, Boston   **155 La Salle St**   **Chicago**

www.ingramcontent.com/pod-product-compliance
Lightning Source LLC
Chambersburg PA
CBHW031355040426

42444CB00005B/295